CHINA IN THE 21st CENTURY

Essays on Key Issues

Ravni Thakur

KALPAZ

ISBN: 978-93-5324-958-8 (PB)

First Published, 2023

Published by

Kalpaz Publications
C-30, Satyawati Nagar,
Delhi – 110052
Ph.: 011-47034999, 9811692060
www.kalpazpublications.com
E-mail: kalpaz@hotmail.com

Printed at: Gyan Press, Delhi.

For my Father
Thakur Harnam Singh (1931-1984)
Founding Director,
Mountaineering Institute, Manali

In everlasting memory

Contents

* Different versions of some articles have been previously published.

Introduction

Fuqiang Guo (rich and powerful) country is a slogan that was popularised by the Chinese reformers of the early twentieth century as they negotiated the huge transformations that were unleashed in China after it lost the Opium Wars starting in 1839. This allowed the entry of British and other western trading companies, ideas and technology into China. This was a cataclysmic event in Chinese history that was to push China into the modern industrial world and into an engagement with the ideas of modernity.

Chinese intellectuals such as Yan Fu (1854- 1921) Li Tachao (1889-1927), Chen Tuxiu (1879-1942), Hu Shi (1891-1962), and especially Mao Zedong (1893-1976), to name a few stalwarts, all blamed China's ossified traditional culture, its lack of modern science and technology, as the main causes for China's loss of status and wealth. While these feelings coalesced into a revolt against the last imperial dynasty of the Manchu's in 1911, unfortunately the Republic that replaced the Manchu's, remained unstable. By the late nineteen-twenties, China was plunged into civil war between a fledgling Communist Party, founded in 1921, and a Nationalist Party led by Jiang Kai–shek (1887-1975), who later went on to be the President of Taiwan. Each espoused a different blueprint for the regeneration of China.

While under Jiang Kai-shek, the KMT turned into a militaristic party, run by the emerging capitalist national bourgeoisie, the Communist Party, followed the lead of the Russian Revolution (1917), and espoused an overthrow of the existing social and political system. The first phase of the civil war was followed by the Sino-Japanese war (1939-44). Japan, empowered by its gains in the First World War, and the success of its earlier industrialisation project, attacked China's Manchuria in 1931 and took over the province, putting in place the country of *Manchuguo* under the erstwhile Manchu Emperor Puyi (1906-1967).

This was the beginning of continual unrest, civil war, and misery in China. Millions were displaced, millions more lost their lives till the Communist Party succeeded in conquering all of China and establishing the People's Republic of China in 1949. Millions more would lose their lives, even as China stabilised as a nation state, led by the Communist Party and Taiwan as an island state under Jiang Kai-shek. In mainland China, the Communist Party remains the source of all power in China. It continues to manage and run the country as it did during the times of Mao.

Mao Zedong was one of the founding members of the Communist Party of China and was appointed the General Secretary of the Party after the Zunyi conference of 1935, and remained so till his death in 1976. Mao was to lay the foundations of a strong single party state on which China's current political and social system is based. His signature goal of land reform and collectivisation was carried out with success and with the killing of millions, designated as class enemies, a category inherited by their children.

Yet after his death, many of Mao's pet ideas, such as a call for permanent revolution and a persistent class war, an opposition to market economics, international trade, communal living and the lifetime system of social guarantees, were simply allowed to die a quiet death. Mao's Great Leap Forward, his great agricultural collectivisation programme of 1958-59, his Cultural Revolution of 1966 were judged as historical mistakes that cost China years and many lives. Instead, Deng Xiaoping (1904-1997), the father of China's economic reform, was to start another revolution. This time a capitalist revolution, that would, in a matter of two decades, transform China from a backward socialist country to one of the leaders of globalisation.

Deng Xiaoping raised his slogan of Four Modernisations in 1978, its goal - to make China a leader in Agriculture, Industry, Defence, Science and Technology, the aim, the same as that of the May Fourth of 1919, to make China into a Fuqiang Guo, a strong and rich country. China has succeeded beyond Deng's expectations. Today, China is the largest world economy in PPP terms, with a GDP of more than 13 trillion US dollars and is a leader in 5 G technology, a space power and a country not afraid to leverage its economic and military might to challenge and change any narratives that hurts the image of China.

In other words, in the 21st century, China is a super power that is challenging America at every step of the way, challenging previous international institutions, creating its own alternatives, backed by its enormous, to paraphrase Nietzche, 'will to power'.

It is a power that is in a position to force compliance form other countries for its goals, whether it be the ambitious Belt and Road Initiative or the manner in which it has expanded its territorial claims in the South China Seas. From Australia to Latin America, from South Asia to Africa, and especially in Europe, China is the largest trading partner of most countries, embedded in their economies like never before. It impacts and, systematically, influences policy decisions in its favour. It is attempting to create a China centric world, putting in place new institutions, and where necessary, taking control over existing institutions, both multilateral and regional. It is the most successful moral, political and military challenge to the two hundred years of western domination.

Deng Xiaoping started cautiously, taking along his conservative colleagues as he turned Maoism on its head and unleashed the entrepreneurial genius of his people, their capacity for hard work and a commitment to making China great again. Since 1961-2, Deng Xiaoping had been associated with the centrist and pragmatist factions of the Party. Liu Shaoqi (1898-1969) and Deng had been responsible for introducing the early attempt at allowing family plots for farmers, especially as Mao's push for collectivisation under the Great Leap Forward of 1958 culminated in unmitigated disaster, with estimates, based on demographic studies, of approximately 30 million peasants starving to death between 1958-61. Deng used Marx to justify his turn to a market economy, pointing out that socialism was always supposed to be a stage after capitalism had been achieved and that the goal of socialism should not be the sharing of poverty but the goal of raising the standards of living of the people. As he famously said, "To get rich is glorious".

The first step was setting up Free Trade zones, the most famous of these being Shenzhen, originally a sleepy village bordering Hong Kong. The aim here was to attract foreign investment and technology through giving cheap land deals, tax rebates and other special privileges for investors. This was China's entry into the world market and was to lead the way in making China a manufacturing capital of the world. Coupled with this was the reintroduction of private family plots in rural China through the introduction of the household responsibility system. In fact, the first rich in China were the 10,000 yuan peasant households being feted by the government by 1983. This was a remarkable change and was meant to encourage both private entrepreneurs and legitimize the role of a market economy. By the late eighties, economic reforms had started to touch urban sector industry with the privatisation and reform of State owned enterprises. Instead of ideology and class, wealth and entrepreneurs were to become the heroes of Deng's China.

Deng's Four Modernisations excluded, and continues to exclude, the fifth modernisation, Democracy as Wei Jingshen, China's first post Mao democracy hero put it when he placed his wall poster on a wall in Beijing in 1978. Instead, Deng promised the Chinese higher standards of living, a return to their private family lives and a partnership with the rest of the world. China's shabby infrastructure, its sleepy towns and villages were to be transformed as odes to modernity, higher, better and smarter than America, better than the West. China opened its door to the West but kept out the 'poisonous weeds and spiritual pollution' of democracy and freedom of expression. It embraced and mastered the intricacy of international trade and breezed on the wings of globalisation to rise like a phoenix, knitting the advanced Western economies into a tight embrace, becoming intrinsic to the supply chains of most manufactured products.

21st century China has arrived. The new Chinese nationalism is not one based on victimhood, tied together through the deliberately elaborated history of a hundred years of humiliation. Today Chinese nationalism is anchored upon an equally deliberately created narrative that highlights China's greatness, ancient and future. It is anchored upon pride and success. It is based on the continuity of the Communist parties control over the levers of all power. China's success, its economic interdependence with the world economy, has allowed China to promote its own system of single party state and efficient control of social dissent. It is this successful China that Xi Jinping leads today. A China that openly espouses a new social, political and economic model in which not the individual but the state is centre stage.

21st century China is also being led by Xi Jingping, considered the strongest CCP leader since Mao Zedong. Since the 18th Party Congress of November 2012, Xi has consolidated his position as the supreme leader for life, succeeding in abrogating the term limits for Chairmanship of the Party set in place by Deng himself when he tried to undo the practice of a Maoist cult.

Xi is indeed a powerful ruler and yet this very power and its centralisation in the body politic of the office of the, now for life, General Secretary of the Communist Party, brings with it its own challenges. China's growth and dominant position in many fields, economic and technological, has also unleashed its own set of contradictions at the international level. Similarly, rising income inequalities within China, a slowing economy and rising unemployment, a growing squeeze of the private sector, all pose grave challenges for the President for life.

In this book we hope to introduce certain key issues in China that it will face as it embraces the 21st century under Xi's rule. We will first look at Xi Jinping's key ideas, his thought and major priorities that are shaping China in the 21st century, with special reference to the revitalisation of the Party. Xi's speeches and their coverage in the main party weekly and papers, show a remarked focus on the central role that Xi thinks the Party should continue to play in China. We will look at what Xi means by his China dream, the term that he has used to describe his vision and hopes for China.

Xi has also made a huge impact on China's foreign policy. China seems to have abandoned Deng's cautious approach of hiding one's strength's and binding one's time. Instead, Xi has taken strong steps to exercise the enormous comprehensive power, economic, military, and political that the country has accumulated, slowly but steadily, since 1978. We will focus on two aspects of his foreign policy. First, the role that China is playing in multilateral organisations by examining BRICS as a multilateral forum since India too is party to this forum. We will then bring out the highlights of Xi's other major foreign policy initiative, his One Belt One Road policy that is both an economic and a foreign policy that aims to further integrate the Chinese economy with those of other countries, sharing a border with China, expanding networks of connectivity, with Europe as the final destination.

Finally, we will look at Chinese society under Xi Jinping. Here the main issue is that of social stratification and inequality, both regional and that of class and access to resources. Two articles, one on social stratification in China, a key internal contradiction today, and another, which is a review article on the politics of development in Tibet and Xinjiang have been included. By the end of the 1990's, scholars such as Sun Liping and others had started to examine the problem of emerging social inequalities in China, amassing masses of data that showed how wealth creation and distribution had not just changed radically but had transformed social relations and the relationship between the CCP led state and society. Market reforms were accompanied by a withdrawal of the earlier social security provisions: health, education, pensions and housing, provided by the state under the *Danwei* or state unit system in urban areas and through the communes and village collectives in rural areas, leaving people without any social security net till social protests forced the state to reorganise social policy in the 1990's. We will examine the dynamics of social stratification to see how Chinese society has changed since economic liberalisation. We will look at the new forms of social inequality and social status that have emerged in China. We will see that China is no longer a society where equality and minimisation of class is the goal.

The article on Tibet examines the politics of development policies and their impact on the lives of the people of Tibet. This article is based on a review of two excellent and detailed books that deal with minority politics in China. Since the late 1980's, China has tried to integrate Tibet and Xinjiang into a tighter economic and political embrace. At the same time, it has touted development as the best manner to engage with this region. Called the development of the western region, these books point out the negative impact that such policies have had on the region and its distinctive culture and religious practices of minority regions.

This book especially includes two essays on specific social groups in China. China's youth and Chinese women. The lives of both have changed radically since 1978. The opportunities available to them and their lifestyles and aspirations have all changed. Based on interviews carried out with university students, this article introduces the new generation of Chinese. Our focus on gender issues highlights the emergence of women's studies in China and how the framing of gender has changed in the recent years. China's return to traditional patterns of gender roles has impacted the lives and opportunities available to Chinese women in a rapidly modernised China. Thus, in this book hopes to outline some of the key issues that will remain with China into the near future and continue to bind its nationhood together.

Finally, we conclude by putting forward an agenda for India to handle the rising economic and geopolitical rise of China. India is China's largest neighbour and has been in a complicated and often adverse position with respect to China. We will argue that for India to maintain its own independence and safeguard itself against China's ambitions, India must deal with China in a pragmatic and long term strategic manner.

PART - I

IDEOLOGY AND KEY INTERNATIONAL POLICIES

Chapter - 1

Xi Jinping and his Thought: The New Ideological Orthodoxy

Brief Biography

Xi Jinping is a fifth generation leader of China, a 'princeling' by birth, that is the elite rulers of China, descended from the pre-liberation communist leadership, party members and Generals from Yenan and the Long March. Xi has seen the vicissitudes of Chinese politics under Mao. Born in 1953, the son of a veteran of the Communist movement and a comrade of Mao Zedong during the civil war of 1944-47, Xi Zhongxun (1913-2002), Xi's early years were spent in relative comfort in special compounds for senior party leaders. Xi's father, a General in the PLA, was also once the deputy Prime Minister of China. The Cultural Revolution of 1966 changed Xi's life and upended his father's career, sending him, like many urban youth, into rural exile. Xi worked in a rural commune in one of China's poorest provinces, Shanxi. He did manual labour and lived with the peasants as one of them. Through the years of his rise, and in many of his policies, one can see that Xi's ideological conviction as a Communist was never to waver.[1]

In 1974, Xi qualified to become a member of the Communist Party and in 1975, he joined China's prestigious Qinghua University in Beijing to study chemical engineering. His father was rehabilitated in 1978. After the death of Mao Zedong in 1976 and the arrest of his wife Jiang Qing and her clique, the Gang of Four, the Cultural Revolution was officially ended and party members and leaders, previously prosecuted or exiled, were rehabilitated and brought back

1. https://www.brookings.edu/wp-content/uploads/2017/10/china_20171013_19thpartycongress_xi_jinping.pdf.

to the center of power. Xi Jinping's father, was soon put in charge of Deng's special project of setting up Free trade zones. Using his father's connections and undoubtedly, his own talent, after his graduation, Xi Jinping got the post of secretary to Geng Biao, the then Minister of National Defence. This was his direct entry into the higher echelons of power[2].

In 1982, Xi left Beijing to become a provincial Party Secretary in the Hebei province. This was to be an important stepping stone for his career development, allowing him to gather direct Party organisational experience and understand the functioning of state governments. From there, he was promoted to Mayor of Amoy city in the province of Fujian. Continuing his steadfast rise, Xi finally became governor of Fujian province in 2000 and did not look back after that. By now Xi had already been identified as someone marked for leadership positions in the central government[3]. By 2007, Xi had been appointed as Party secretary of Shanghai, replacing the previous Secretary who was removed for corruption. Party Secretary in Shanghai, China's richest and most cosmopolitan city was certainly a clear indication that Xi would make it to Beijing and in October of 2007, Xi had been appointed to the post of Vice-President of China, and earmarked as a serious contender to take over from Hu Jintao in 2013. By 2010, he was also elected vice-Chairman of the Military commission, the second most important body after the Party and one that ensured leadership over the armed forces.

In the Seat of Power

In 2012, Xi was elected as General Secretary of the Party and in 2013, President of the country. In short, Xi was in full control.[4] This control was re-enforced during the Third Plenum of 2013[5]. Third Plenums are important events in China since they come during the second year of the newly appointed General Secretary. They also reflect the consolidation of power that occurs during this period in the person of the General Secretary. Often, this changeover is preceded by

2. Kerry Brown (2017), *CEO of China: The Rise of Xi Jinping*, IB Tauris.
3. *Ibid.*
4. *Ibid.*
5. China Focus: 19th CPC Central Committee 3rd plenum issues communique *Source:* Xinhua| 2018-03-01 01:36:53|.

inner party struggles and whispers in the corridors of power. Analysts comment that two major factions can broadly be identified. One, those who are dubbed Princelings. The other group is seen as those who are first generation or come from smaller political families and have made their way through the youth wings of the Party, such as Hu Yaobang or Wen Jiabao and now Li Keqiang, the current Prime Minister who rose through the ranks and through membership of the Youth League from 2004-2008[6] Xi Jinping, although representing the Princelings, is acceptable to the reformists in the Party because of his support for reform, to the Military because of his father and his wife, Peng Lijian, who is an officer and famous singer in the PLA, and to the conservatives because of his support for a strong state and the leading role of the Party.

Read within the ambit of domestic politics, the 1978 Third Plenum, when the levers of power were handed over to Deng Xiaoping, remains the most important and has meant the rise of the moderate wing within the Communist party, one that represented fundamental change in the ideology and policies of China[7]. Since then, every plenum has only added to this turn towards a market economy and greater opening to the world. Of course the main focus is to chart out the broad vision of the new General Secretary.

The 60 point **Decision on Several Major Questions on Deepening Reform,** issued after the plenum, reflects the importance that the Xi leadership attaches to particular issues. The main theme of the plenum was its renewed commitment to the 'primacy of the market'. The overall goal till 2020 is clearly stated as the following:

> In the face of new circumstances and new tasks, in order to comprehensively construct a moderately prosperous society and thereby create a wealthy, strong, democratic, harmonious and civilised socialist country and realise the Chinese dream of the great rejuvenation of the Chinese nation, reform must be comprehensively deepened from a new historical point.[8]

6. Elizabeth Economy (2018), *The Third Revolution: Xi Jinping and the New Chinese State,* Oxford.
7. Shambaugh, David, (2016), *China's Future*, Polity Press.
8. China Focus: 19th CPC Central Committee 3rd plenum issues communique *Source:* Xinhua| 2018-03-01 01:36:53|

This statement clearly brings out Xi's own aims for his reign. The key words here are wealthy and strong, harmonious and of course socialist. Wealthy implies that the market economy will remain in place, strong is a nod to the role that technology and the military will play in ensuring China's international position and harmonious can be read as a nod, to both China's traditional Confucian ethos, and a signal that anything that disturbs this harmony, dissent and challenges to the Communist party, will not be tolerated. The other key word used here is "moderately prosperous society". This has become a key ideological tool that is also destined to address the huge social inewualities and wealth disparities existing in China today. It is this idea of common prosperity that has allowed him to create a pro poor image.

One of the most famous stories about Xi comes from a statement he made during one of the annual Beidaihe meetings of senior Chinese leaders. This is a famous sea side resort, not far from Beijing, where traditionally, the leaders of the CCP retreated for a summer break. It is here that they discuss and make decisions that will influence the lives of millions. After his appointment as General Secretary, during the meeting held in Beidaihe, Xi is supposed to have disparaged the loss of power of the Soviet Union and the Russian Communist Party. As he is quoted to have said in 2012, just after being nominated to the highest post in the Party:

> Why did the Soviet Union disintegrate? Why did the Soviet Communist Party collapse? An important reason was that their ideals and convictions wavered[9] .

Xi Jinping and the CCP leadership has learnt a lot from the fall of the Soviet Empire. Above all, they decided that the leadership of the Communist Party had to be saved at all costs and Xi seems to have made that his major goal. To ensure the leadership of the Party, Xi has proceeded to cut to size all other social and political institutions. According to Xi, it is the Party and the Party alone that can lead China into the future and the only institution that can guarantee peace and prosperity. In fact, that has been Xi's primary influence and all the

---

9. Katzuchi Nakazawa: Nikkei Asia: 2020 O.Conner, Sean (2018), "SOE's Megamergers signal new direction in China's Economy", US China Economy and Security Review Commission, 24 May https://www.uscc. gov/sites/default/files/ Research/SOE% 20Megamergers.pdf

measures taken by him since his ascendancy, have been calculated to ensure that the CCP remains the unchallenged ruler of China.

The 'Core' of the Party 党的核心 (Dang de hexin)

Xi proceeded to consolidate his personal position by launching his first signature campaign, the Anti-corruption campaign that was to signal his intent as a disciplinarian[10]. Not only did this campaign target and eliminate his main competitors such as Bo Xilai, the erstwhile governor of Chongqing and Zhou Yongkang, the erstwhile social security chief, but also put fear in the hearts of all his party colleagues as he appointed Wang Qishan, said to be the closest to him, to lead this drive targeting what he called both the 'tigers and the flies'[11]. This campaign was also a signal to the masses of cadre and business men of China that it was not going to be business as usual. The decades of relative freedom and openness was about to turn.

Further cementing Xi's role as the "core of the Party", was Xi's leadership of several small leading groups that were designed and especially created to oversee and centralise all decision making. The Leading Small Groups ((*lingdao xiaozu*, 领导小组),. These leading groups oversee decision making and are the final authority. Now Xi heads 8 of them, the others headed by his supporters within the Politburo and the Central Committee, further centralising decision making, even within the existing leadership[12]. Nothing exemplifies Xi's control over the Republic than the enshrining of *Xi Jinping Thought* as part of the Chinese Constitution. This puts Xi in the same league as Mao and Deng, telling its citizens that a challenge to Xi and his ideas is also a challenge to China's constitution.[13]

---

10. Hough, Dan, "Is China still on the Anti Corruption Road to Nowhere despite Xi Jinping's Campaign", *South China Morning Post,* 25 Jan 2020.
11. Xi Jinping vows to fight "tigers and flier in anti-corruption fight" *The Guardian, Jan* 22, 2013. https://www.theguardian.com/world/2013/jan/22/xi-jinping-tigers-flies-corruption
12. Johnson, Christopher K (2017), "Innovation: The Rise of Leading Small Groups", in CSIS Centre for Strategic & International Studies, October 17 https:// www.csis.org/analysis/xis-signature-governance-innovation-rise-leading-small-groups
13. Buckley, Chris (2017), "China Enshrines Xi Jinping Thought: What does that Mean", in *New York Times*, 24 October https://www.nytimes.com/2017 /10/24/world/asia/china-xi-jinping-constitution.html

Two volumes of his ideas, largely composed of his talks and speeches at various institutions and occasions, have become compulsory reading and are even available through a special social media app. Reams of newspaper print, academic papers and conferences have been held to publicise and project Xi as the 'Core' of the Party, again a title given to Mao. And it is to Party organisation, party ideology and party primacy that Xi has devoted a great deal of his attention[14].

No Communist Party, No New China

Xi's birth in a strongly Red household and his own positions as Party Secretary at the provincial level, must have instilled in him the much touted slogan from the times of Mao. "If there was no Communist Party, there would be no New China" (*meiyou gongchandang meiyou xin Zhongguo*), an essential belief needed to justify and strengthen the Party's continued role in national governance.

Since its foundation in 1922, the CCP has seen many internal struggles, both over power and at the ideological level. China watchers dubbed this the two line theory, one representing the centrists that saw the need for a certain measure of markets and also believed in the necessity of western technology to raise the levels of China's own productive forces. This moderate line, opposed to Maoist radicalism and represented by Liu Shaoqi and Deng Xiaoping, was linked to the old dream, the desire for western technology and a Chinese soul. This underpinned Deng Xiaoping's strategy as he opened to the West and its technology while admonishing the Chinese state to "hide its strengths and bide its time."[15] This, he rightly assessed as the best way to allay western fears about the rise of China.

Xi Jinping has inherited a China that has succeeded in its goals and where the struggle over the correct line to follow with regard to western trade and technology has long been resolved. The wealth that has come into China, the emergence of a strong and vibrant private sector, has also brought challenges to the ideology and relevance of both Marxism as a world view and the need of a Communist Party to govern the nation that now boasts of a booming middle class

14. Shambaugh (2016), *op.cit.*
15. Richard Javaad Haydarian (2014), "Hide you strengths and bide your time," in https://www.aljazeera.com/opinions/2014/11/21/hide-your-strength-bide-your-time/

consumerism and wealth seeking. The collapse of the Soviet empire and the loss of status suffered by Russia, convinced the leadership of Deng that the CCP was necessary for the stability of China[16]. Xi's challenge is to balance a communist ideology with the presence of billionaires and reconcile the ideology with its practice.

Challenging the Party's Narrative

Since the death of Mao, the greatest challenge to the rule of the Communist Party came in 1989, when students, workers and ordinary office goers, common people all joined a month long movement in the heart of Beijing's famous Tian Anmen square to demand Democracy, the one battle that the Chinese people have always lost since the aborted Republic of 1911. Tian Anmen represented a turning point. Masses of people had gathered throughout the month of March 1989 to protest against the hegemony of the Communist Party, the emergence of crony capitalism and corruption and above all, the lack of freedom of expression. Wuer Kaixi, one of the leaders of the student movement and the one who debated the Prime Minister on Television, describes in graphic detail, the terrible massacre that occurred on the night of the 3- 4 of June and its aftermath[17].

Zhao Ziyang, the then Prime Minister's biography **Prisoner of State**[18]**,** the secret journal of Premier Zhao Ziyang (1919-2005) makes interesting reading as it points out the huge divide that occurred between the hardliners and the reformists during this period, the new two line being not about economic policy but the degree to which democracy and civil society should be allowed to play a role in China. The reformists were led by Zhao and the disciples of Hu Yaobang, who had died, but had led the youth league entrants into the higher echelons of power. The reformists had argued for greater democracy and freedom while the hardliners, led by Li Peng and those dubbed as the inheritors of the mantle of their fathers, the Princelings, felt that any challenge to the Communist Party must be quashed mercilessly. Tanks rolled into Tian Anmen, squashing the democracy activists like ants.

16. Cheng Li (2017), *China's New Politburo and Members of the Politburo*, Brookings Institute, October 25, 2017.
17. Wuer Kaixi (1990), "Tianan Men and Beyond: After the Massacre", *Journal of Democracy,* Winter, Vol. 1. Issue 1. pp. 6-8.
18. Zhao Ziyang (2005), *Prisoner of the State: The Secret Journal of Zhao Ziyang*, Simon and Schutser.

Thousands lost their lives, thousands escaped along the underground network to relive and speak about the horrors of the night of April 3rd and 4th. Zhao Ziyang lost his job and was placed under house arrest till the day he died. His memoirs were smuggled out and published after his death[19]. With the tragedy of Tian Anmen, China once again lost its battle for democracy and many young lost their lives.

However, Deng Xiaoping did learn a lesson. The need for reform was not in the relationship that the party had with the people but the intra party relations and reform that was needed. Under Deng's early guidance the Party was to transform from one made up of workers, peasants and soldiers to one that would be made up of educated and qualified technocrats, able to lead China's charge and co-opted the Party as gainers of China's rapid modernisation and its entry into the world as economic decision makers[20]. The party opened its doors to other classes under the leadership of Jiang Zemin, who promulgated the *Theory of Three represents* that reemphasised the key role of the Party as the indisputable leader of China but allowed those not from the 'right' classes, such as entrepreneurs to also enter the Party.[21]

Jiang and his successor, Hu Jintao, continued to largely follow the policy framework and balance between ideological rigidity and CCP rule. A focus on class contradictions and class war was downgraded by bringing out the slogan of a harmonious society, legitimizing tacitly, China's pre-Communist Confucian ideas, based on harmony[22]. They continued to deepen economic reform, moved to integrate China in all international organisations but still maintain a non-threatening international profile. The leadership realised that the people had to be taken along and a large number of social freedoms, such as the right to travel, greater academic freedom, interactions and exchange with international academics, the large scale transformation of the urban

19. Alan P.L. Liu (1990), Aspects of Beijing's Crisis Management: The Tiananmen Square Demonstration, *Asian Survey* Vol. 30, No. 5, pp. 505-521.
20. Dickson, Bruce J (2008), *Wealth and Power: The Communist Parties Embrace of the Private Sector*, Cambridge University Press.
21. China Daily, "Three Represents", July 10, 2007 https://www.chinadaily. com.cn/china/2007-07/10/content_6142053.htm
22. Choukroune, Leila and Antoine Garapon (2007), "The Norms of Chinese Harmony: Disciplinary Rules as Social Stabiliser", in *China Perspectives* No. 3 pp. 36-49.

landscape and a vibrant economy, helped paper over the fissures and contradictions unleashed by the Tian Anmen movement[23].

The nineties and the early decade of the 20th century were the period of China's greatest prosperity, when it went all out to become a commanding international economy. It transformed the lives of its people by large investments in infrastructure and it identified clear priorities such as technology and cyber and space sectors. Greater freedom was also allowed in the media, and with the academic communities. This period saw a burgeoning of the social sciences in China as Chinese universities invested heavily in new staff and technologies to enter the top tier of international universities. Chinese scholars carried out excellent primary research to document the enormous changes that were taking place in China. It is largely through their work and research that western scholars were able to appreciate the full extent and transformation of China's political economy[24].

While millions were pulled out of poverty and cities became places with gleaming towers and shopping malls, many were to also fall through the cracks in a state capitalist system that now defined China. The workers and peasants, the millions of migrant labour without security began to form a new underclass, causing social protests and unrest. In its desire to catch up with the West and even to surpass it, China compromised on many things, chiefly the massive social security net that iron rice bowl, a life time of support that Mao had guaranteed under his Communist revolution. For the masses, the Party was no longer a party of the masses, it was a party that accumulated wealth and privilege for its members and was seen as steeped in corruption. This is something that the author witnessed personally in her constant travels to China during this period.

The youth of that time were also responding to the calls for Glasnost and Perestroika that were emanating from Russia and the erstwhile Soviet Empire In fact, the demonstrations first started during Gorbachev's visit to Beijing in the autumn of the previous year. All around them, Communism and Communist parties seemed to have had their day. China was the last man standing. And it was

23. Hong Shi (1990), "China's Political Development after Tiananmen: Tranquility by Default"*Asian Survey,* Vol. 30, No. 12, pp. 1206-121.
24. Thakur (2007), "Social Sciences in China: Sociology as a Subject", in Madhvi Thampi (ed). *Chinese Studies in India*, Institute of Chinese Studies.

for this mission "to guard the rule of the Communist Party" that Deng Xiaoping ordered the tanks to march into Tianan Men. It is the same mission that guides Xi Jinping's increasing authoritarianism and his emphasis on strengthening and disciplining a party that has lost the legitimacy to rule. It is in this context and against this background that we must look at some of Xi Jinping's major policy imperatives.

Reasserting Party Control

One of the most prominent aspects of Xi Jinping thought has been his concerted efforts to recreate the central and primary position of the Communist Party in the governance of Chinese politics and society. As he said:

> It is a great blessing for China, the Chinese people and the Chinese nation to have the CPC as the ruling party. As long as we read and understand the history of modern China and that of the revolution, it is readily apparent that without the leadership of the CPC, our nation would never have made such progress, nor would we have achieved such high international standing. In maintaining the fundamental principle of upholding the Party's leadership, we should be particularly sober minded and keen sighted and take a firm stand, allowing no ambiguity (Dec 11, 2015).

This reemphasis on the unquestioning leadership of the party and the basic tenets of Marxist ideology has been one of Xi's clear aims. He has asserted this primacy of the party at every forum, including the armed forces. As Kawazaka points out, one of the slogans ratified at the party's last national congress, in 2017, was "Party, government, military, civilian, and academic; east, west, south, north, and center, the Party leads everything."[25]

This reflects the strict ideological line that Xi has taken with regard to any challenges to the Party and any dissent that questions the right of the Party to govern China. He has reinforced ideological control over all means of social messaging and academic discussion. The leadership of Xi firmly believes that only the CCP stands between China and chaos and has moved towards a degree of hard authoritarianism.

---

25. Kawazaka: *op.cit.*

Xi did not stop at only controlling the party cadre. The effort was to exercise oversight over all academic and opinion making activities. Any criticism of the Party decisions, and especially, any criticism of Xi himself, were brought under the scanner. A quasi independent media, academic and research, were all to suffer increasing controls. Any attempt to tarnish the image of the Party was to be met with firm action, and in recent years, this has meant the incarceration of several journalists and intellectuals. These include human rights lawyers, representing workers whose wages have not been paid, or peasants dispossessed of their land without compensation. It has also included students, feminists, environmentalists and artists like Ai Weiwei, human rights activists like Liu Xia.[26] The most recent arrests have included students of elite universities who designated themselves as Marxists, claiming to stand for a genuine Marxism that was allied with working class interests and not that of developers or the new millionaires of China.

The Communist Party's attempts to control all narratives about its history and politics has not stopped within its borders. In order to save the party's face and especially that of Xi Jinping, journalists and publishers have been picked up from Hong Kong, appearing days later to admit to the charges against them. Further, more and more evidence illustrates how China is using its overseas students and workers to spy on each other and collectively challenge and denigrate any news that targets the CCP[27]. China has also made extensive use of its social media bots to propagandize amongst its own people and attempt to influence international public opinion. Of course, control and censorship of all internet platforms is a given. China has an army of youngsters whose only job is to scour the internet for any anti-China propaganda and block it. They also target bloggers who raise questions about Chinese policies and government.[28]

26. Ma, Alexander (2018), "How China Deals with Dissidence", in *Business Insider*, August 19, 2018.
27. Anders Corr, "Chinese Informants In The Classroom: Pedagogical Strategies", *Forbes*, Jun 28, 2017,08:31am EDT, https://www. forbes.com/sites/ anderscorr/ 2017/06/28/ chinese-informants-in-the-classroom-pedagogical-strategies/#4df25f0e12da
28. Heavan, Douglas (2019), "China's Great Firewall and the War to Control the Internet", in *New Scientist*, 12 March, https://www.newscientist. com/article/ mg24132210-400-chinas-great-firewall-and-the-war-to-control-the-internet/

China has succeeded in creating an Orwellian technological surveillance apparatus that covers everything. The internet of everything is also the internet of everything under surveillance. More importantly, China has now put in place a system of total surveillance that is also meant to create a data base of 'good citizens'. Any laws broken, from spitting on the street to speeding are now recorded against a score card that can determine your travel rights, access to loans and overall freedom.[29] This leveraging of technology to monitor its citizenship has always existed but under Xi Jinping they have become more overt and draconian.

The Anti-Corruption Drive

Xi has also stressed the need to clean up the Party and burnish the Party's image by weeding out all those elements and actions that harm the public image of the Party. Corruption amongst Party members has been one of his chief concerns, as brought out by *Qiushi*, China's official Party daily. It was amongst the first to bring out the official analysis and imperatives of Xi Jinping thought in a special issue of Jan-March 2017. The issue gives a full text of the special ordinance on Regulations of the Communist Party of China on Internal Oversight. As the resolution says:

> The CPC's internal oversight represents an important part of Party building, and an important foundation for comprehensively governing the Party with strict discipline...We have strictly enforced political discipline and political rules and resolutely curbed the spread of corruption. (p.7)

This anti-corruption campaign has become Xi Jinpings key campaign, designed to show to the people that the CCP leadership will no longer tolerate corruption and any other anti-party activities, Senior leaders like Bo Xilai, the Party Chief of Chongqing and at one time considered a rival to Xi Jinping, also a Princeling, was the first to fall. He is still in prison and will, in all probability, die there. The second big gun to fall was Zhou Yongkang, once the Minister for internal security and again, a challenge to Xi, since he knew where all the skeletons were. He too is still in prison.

29. Mitchell, Anna and Larry Diamond (2019), "China's Surveillance State should scare everyone", in *The Atlantic*, 2018/02.

Apart from handling his rivals, Xi's campaign swept through the party like a juggernaut, sweeping up more than 1,000,000 cadres, both big and small. Generals from the military, long used to a degree of independence and luxury were not spared either, with several finding themselves behind bars. As Xi Jinping has said himself" People resent corruption. Corruption could lead to the downfall of the Party and the State" (2010). Between 2012 and 2014, the Central Commission for Discipline Inspection investigated more than 400,000 cadre at different levels, the tigers and the flies. It also repatriated more than 1,200 cadre serving in different positions abroad. Since then, the campaign has only accelerated and become a fearsome tool for garnering loyalty and strict adherence to the Party line being articulated from the very top.[30]

The campaign has served a two-fold purpose. First, it ensured that any challenge to Xi's rule and authority was quashed and that the party as a whole fell in line with his way of thinking. The second goal was to show to the masses that in the future, nobody would be considered above the law, even if they were *gaoji ganbu* or senior leaders, their family and or the ordinary grass root cadres. Zhou Xinmin attributes two major achievements of Jinping's disciplinary and anti-corruption drive. These are first, elevating political discipline to and rules to a paramount position and maintaining a constant oversight of party bureaucrats through inspection tours and other form of peer surveillance. Second, creating confidence amongst Party cadre that they are on the right path.[31] These actions were meant to tell the people that Xi was firmly in charge and that their biggest grievance against the Party, its corruption would be handled on a war footing. Where the people were concerned, it certainly helped Xi create an image of strength and righteousness as the legitimate leader of China. His anti-corruption drive has been accompanied by a massive propaganda push declaring Xi as the core of the party and the country.

People's Liberation Army answers to the Party

Apart from social and political control of the general public, Xi

30. Fiol Mahon (2018), "Xi Jinping's anti-corruption drive: The Hidden Motives of a Modern Day Mao", Foreign Policy Research Institute, August 17.
31. Zhou Xinmin (2017), *Xi Jinping's Governance and the Future of China*, Skyhorse Publishers, New York.

has also reiterated the Party's primacy over the armed forces. As he has said several times, the army must be loyal to the Party.

> The military should uphold Party spirit and principles. Belief in Party spirits and principles is the fundamental quality of Party members as well as the fundamental requirements of our political work. In doing our work, we must put the principles cause of our Party and the interests of our people first. A Party members we must love the Party, protect the Party, work for the Party and share weal and woe with the Party.[32]

From the very beginning, the CCP was a party that was both a military and a political party. Since 1927 and the formation of the short lived Jiangxi Soviet, the military and armed forces have been an intrinsic component of the communist struggle. Mao's famous slogan, "Power flows through the barrel of a gun", was a real slogan, not just one for effect. The eighth route army and its transformation into the People's Liberation Army was an ideological mainstay. The army in turn, especially after the Long March, and during the Yenan period, was composed largely of peasants from the so called liberated areas.[33]

Several articles and films have been written in recent years to once again remind the masses of the heroism of Communist soldiers. As a recent article in the *Qiushi* puts it:

> The Long March was not only a process of overcoming the enemy, clinching a victory and achieving a strategic goal but was also a process of developing new theories and exploring a revolutionary path on the basis of actual conditions.[34]

Thus, the success and ideology of Maoism is closely tied, not to the idea of a Bolshevik revolution, but to that of a peasant army that developed special tactics to defeat forces superior in numbers.

This revolutionary history is constantly reiterated to strengthen the bond between the two institutions and to emphasize their oneness. The CCP and its armed wing are inseparable. It is for this

32. Xi Jinping (2017), *Explanation on the Code of Conduct for Intraparty Political Life under New Circumstances and the Regulations of the Communist Party of China on Internal Oversight*", Qiushi, Vol. 9, No. 1, Issue no. 30, pp. 3-15.
33. Selden, Mark (1971), *The Yenan Way*, Harvard University Press.
34. Qiushi, *op.cit,* p. 20.

reason that the General Secretary of the CCP is also simultaneously the Chairman of the Military Commission, its overall commander. Under Xi Jinping, the relative freedom and independence given to the higher echelons of the Military brass, especially those above the rank of General, has been curtailed and they too have been brought under the direct disciplinary control of the Party.[35]

The CCP does not believe in the separation of powers between the executive, legislature or the judiciary. The function of each institution is to defend and safeguard the Party above all else. In other words the armed wing of the party continues to be its guarantor in power. The article further goes on to state:

> A person without a spirit cannot stand tall. A country without a spirit cannot be strong, A spirit is the essence on which people depend on for their long term survival...The spirit of the long march is an important constituent of the Chinese communists Red heritage has been deeply suffused into the veins and history of the Chinese nation.[36]

It is this constant equating of nationalism with the Communist spirit, that too of struggle and war, that has defined modern history as the Chinese people learn it. Any one questioning this heritage is designated as traitorous. The nation, the Party and the Chinese people are supposed to be one. The state is the people, not an institution meant to be questioned. Xi, has of course, gained trust from the army by modernising it with high tech investments, restructuring numbers of infantry and further allowing it to exercise its muscles in the South China Seas. A recent detailed report on the subject provides us with the latest advances in China's defence preparedness and postures. It shows a rapidly expanding naval and technological advance in recent years, designed to challenge and maintain its power and superiority in the South China Seas and beyond into the Pacific.[37] The military is seen as an important component of China's Dream to become a

35. Youji (2018), "Xi Jinping and PLA Transformation through Reforms", RSIS Working Paper, No. 313, May 21. *https://www.jstor. org/stable/ resrep19922?seq=1#metadata_info_tab_contents*
36. Qiushi (2017) , *op.cit,* p. 21.
37. Defense Intelligence Agency (2019), "China's Military Power: Modernizing a Force to Win", Report https://www.dia.mil/Portals/27/ Documents/News/Military%20 Power%20 Publications/China_Military_Power_FINAL_5MB_20190103.pdf

world leader and reemphasizing the key leadership of the CCP over the armed forces, not just secures the Party but also provides the real force behind its survival. Today, it is also seen as essential for China to weather the blowback coming its way from the United States.

Marxism and Ideological Correctness

At the same time, the philosophy of Marxism has been pushed as the main component of Chinese social sciences. Outlining the need for social sciences and philosophy to learn from three main sources, Marxism, the best of Chinese culture and the best of foreign ideas. As Xi himself puts it:

> Marxist resources: These include sections of Marxism, the achievements of adapting Marxism to the Chinese context and its cultural manifestations – The CPC, theories, guidelines, principles and policies, the path, theoretical systems and institutions.... These constitute the primary substance of philosophy and social sciences of Chinese of Chinese features. They also constitute the fastest growing areas in Chinese philosophy.[38]

Thus, although space is given to other sources of knowledge and experience, there is no doubt that questioning of Marxist philosophy and methodologies will not be tolerated at the academic levels in China's universities and academic discourse. As Xi said while commemorating Marx's bicentennial anniversary.

We commemorate Marx as the greatest thinker in human history and also to declare our firm belief in scientific Marxism (4 May: 2018).

According to the South China Morning Post, Xi actually led the Politburo in a study circle to discuss the Communist Manifesto.[39] Political classes in schools and colleges have always been compulsory but now their importance is linked to the overall grades of students and the manner in which their future loyalty to the state and party will be assessed. It will determine the trajectory of their success[40]. This also includes what Economy has called the 'No's' of teaching and

---

38. Xi Jinping (2017 edition), *The Governance of China,* Vol. 1, p. 371, People's Publishing House.
39. Gan, N (2018), "A New Class Struggle: China's party workers get back to the basics", *South China Morning Post*, 29 April, 2015.
40. *Ibid.*

debate. "No to democracy, freedom of expression and or any western value systems".[41]

Many China watcher have argued that Xi is a throwback to Mao and a conservative Marxist, determined to pull back on democratic reform and any attempt to seek any semblance of freedom of expression[42]. But Xi is not Mao. While he has once again premised the success of his regime on the continuation of Communist rule and has pushed an authoritarian agenda against civil society, he does believe in Deng's market economy, international trade and in the glory of riches. But unlike Deng, Xi does not believe that the Party must play a greater role in good governance and less in ideological warfare.

Deng wanted to balance the Party with capitalism. Xi, on the other hand, believes that a market economy's only purpose is to allow the Communist party to benefit from globalisation and its access to knowledge and technology. He believes that State owned enterprises must once again lead the economy and continue to hold primacy in China. The expanded role of the state in a market economy, rather than private sector growth is the basic principle of market socialism.[43] Thus, Xi's aim has been to re-centre the Party as the continued fulcrum of Chinese governance and at the same time ensure greater accountability and ideological conformity.

At the level of Party schools, Marxist studies and ideological self awareness are also being stressed. A rich China under Xi will still be a communist China. This has belied the hope of the western liberals who had presumed and hoped that China's increased integration in the capitalist world economy would also induce a process of democratic politics, leading to the end of a single party Communist state.

The increased centralisation and surveillance is not necessarily a positive step. How this impacts entrepreneurship and the flexibility enjoyed by regional and business leaders earlier, may also impact the economy. The constant fear of surveillance by your peers and now by China's new technology, can hardly be conducive to decision making.

41. Economy: *op cit.*
42. Blanchette Jude (2019), *China's New Redguards: The Return of Radicalism and the return of Mao Zedong*, Oxford University Press.
43. Barry Naughton (2017), "Is China Socialist?", in *The Journal of Economic Perspectives,* Vol. 31, No. 1 (Winter 2017), pp. 3-24.

One of the best boosters for the economy under Deng Xiaoping was the freedom of states to compete, to innovate and make rapid decisions. This decentralisation helped stimulate China's growth and gave rise to a class of innovative entrepreneurs. It also allowed Western companies to feel comfortable in building their own networks and contact. Today, there is significant evidence that the Party is controlling the huge social media following and popularity of business entrepreneurs, film stars, intellectuals and others who earlier have challenged the Party's dominance and provided alternatives for the youth of China an alternative role model for advancement and self growth and upward social mobility than the Party[44].

Message for the People: The China Dream and Nationalism

Despite the rather romantic use of the word dream, Xi Jinpings China Dream is essentially a message for the people and is firmly grounded in material reality. Put simply, the overall goal of the China dream is to raise the standard of living of all Chinese and by 2050, create a largely middle class society, while inculcating in them the feeling of "communist" nationalism. As the article says:

> "The "Chinese Dream" proposed by President Xi Jinping depicts a blueprint for an expanding middle class in China, which is crucial for China's economic transition and will boost the global economy[45].

Nationalism is not new to China. China is the oldest nation state in the world that has had written records going back to 1500 BCE and earlier. Nationalism, if defined as a construction of a comprehensive culture and tradition as sources of a common identity, and shared destiny, has always existed. By the first century, China boasted of a moral scaffolding of Confucian practices and philosophy that would continue to govern the Han, the original ethnic group from the Yellow river basin and help them define their country as *Zhongguo* or the Middle kingdom[46].

44. Griffith, James (2019), *The Great Firewall of China: How to build and control an alternative version of the Internet,* Zed Books.
45. "Chinese Dream Depicts blueprint for middle class", *Xinhua*, China Daily, Updated: 2013-11-16 14:56 (Xinhua).
46. For an overview of Chinese History, see the updated edition of John K. Fairbank and Merle Goldman (2006), *China A New History*, Harvard University Press.

Modern nationalism is often associated with the rise of nation states as defined territorial entities. In China, it was defined by two main discourses, one the failure of China to compete with the West and two, laying the failure at the doorstep of the Manchu dynasty, China's last dynasty, seen as foreign since they were not of Han ethnicity (1644-1911). Chinese history exhibits a great deal of continuity in its forms of dominant political system and Confucian ideas. China's two conquerors, the Mongols and especially the Manchu's, appropriated and continued with the Confucian bureaucratic state governance system run by China's literate elite. The Communists, as a western ideological force, have been no different, adapting to the specificities of Chinese culture and its historical legacy of centralised governance structures and authority[47].

Sun Yat-sen and his Guomindang party that led the 1911 republican revolution against the Manchu's, took from western modernist discourse and anchored their aspirations in modeling China's Republic along the lines of western political democracy, with free trade, science and technology, as the agents of transformation. The project of modernisation was synonymous with industrialisation and the development of a manufacturing industry. Unfortunately, this early dream of a republican democracy was a failure and Sun died in 1925, paving the way for a return to a more authoritarian rule of one man, Jiang Kai-shek[48].

However, to paraphrase Benedict Anderson, the 1911 revolution did transform the 'idea of the nation' and overnight the dominant discourse became one that derided and looked down on its own past, seeing in its rigorous adherence to form and custom, the ossification of Chinese culture. For intellectuals of this era, from about 1870 onwards, the Nation meant being modern, being equal in the science and technology, the new world of knowledge that made up the industrial and colonial enterprise.

This period also sees a third conceptualisation of what a nation state should be. Nationalism included a New Culture Movement that sought to overturn and destroy all the old structures and institutions

47. *Ibid*
48. For an excellent overview of this period and the governance and life of Jiang Kai-Shek, see David Fenby (2005), Chiang Kai-Shek: China's Generalissimo and the China he Lost, De Capo Press.

of traditional China. For this group, the imagined community drew its inspiration from the Marxist cannon and the 1917 proletarian revolution in Russia. The Communists believed in an international government that would be based on the victory of the working classes as they rose up against the exploitation of the then dominant class, the capitalist enemy.

This meant, first and foremost, the setting up of communist parties the world over under the leadership by the Soviet created Comintern. The Chinese communist party was set up in 1921 and its leadership was encouraged to form an united front with the already existing Guo Mindang Party led by Sun Yat-sen. Sun was declared the President of this united front government and the goal of this alliance was to defeat the forces of colonialism and imperialism, the word given by Lenin to define the economics of colonialism.[49] This alliance was doomed to failure, the ideas of a nation and its goals, too radically apart, for the future of China. The ideological conflicts were to translate into military conflict and China was ravaged by war throughout the first four decades of the twentieth century.

The idea of a Modern nation state, really takes shape only after the Communist party comes to power in 1949. It is a rather simple and comprehensive nationalism, this time tied to the Communist Party's leadership role. The new regime created new histories, and its modern history starts with the rise of the communist party, and its new mythical heroes are communist heroes. Under Mao, the goal of this new history was a world revolution, a permanent revolution to guard against the betrayal of the post Stalinist Kruschev period in Russia and to counter his own enemies within China. Mao felt the mantle of the revolution and its safety now lay with him.[50]

A major part of this new history and new nationalism has been the narrative of a 'hundred years of humiliation', starting from the Opium Wars of 1839-42 and the unequal treaties that reduced China's

49. For an excellent book with new data and insights, see Yoshihiro, Ishikawa (2013), *The Formation of the Chinese Communist Party*, (translated by Joshua A. Fogel) Columbia University Press.
50. Jung Chang and Jon Halliday have given us a version of Mao that highlights his egotistical and often emperor like tendencies. They show Mao as wanting to be the new and unquestioned leader of China and the Communist world. See their (2005), *Mao The Untold Story*, Jonathan Cape.

status in the world to a semi-colony. It was after the stability achieved under the CCP in 1949 that China start moving towards its own revival. Communist nationalism meant ensuring that this 'century of humiliation' is never repeated and China's rise as a world power in the 21st century justifies the system of Communist government.[51] This history of victimhood also allows the Chinese CCP to claim the true nationalist mantle since it is the Party that succeeded in changing China from the poor man of Asia to the second largest economy in the world.

Under Deng Xiaoping and his drive to open up China and attract foreign investments and technology, China's nationalism was low key and understated. China stressed its concept of peaceful rise and its desire for common prosperity. However, in recent years, China's nationalist propaganda has become more strident. As China's economic and military power rises, Xi Jinping has attempted to fuse a spirit of nationalism into his concept of China Dream. The China Dream includes in it a revival of China's original great civilisation, its ancient art, inventions and cultural achievements. It is this restoration of China's true greatness that makes the China Dream.

Here, Xi is not doing anything differently from what actually starts under Jiang and Hu, and that is the revalidation of traditional Chinese culture while modernising it to take its 'rightful place amongst the comity of nations'. It is commonly said that, "Mao made us stand up, Deng made us rich and now Xi is going to make us strong. "*(Mao ba women zhanqi lai le, Deng ba women fu qilai le he Xi ba women qiangqi laile)*[52].

Xi himself is quoted as saying:

> The people are the creators of history...The extensive and profound Chinese civilisation was created by the Chinese people. The spirit of the Chinese nation...The endeavour of the Chinese people has led to the tremendous

51. Townsend, James (1992), "Chinese Nationalism", in *The Australian Journal of Chinese Affairs*. No. 27 (Jan., 1992), pp. 97-130.
52. Mu Xuequan Xi stresses unity, striving for national rejuvenation at PRC anniversary reception, 2019-09-30 23:38:40 http://www.xinhuanet. com/english/2019-09/30/c_138437557. htm. The saying is broadly repeated on the streets and in general discussions with Chinese friends.

> transformation of the Chinese nation. It has stood up, grown rich and become strong....People are desiring great unity...they are a people with a great spirit for pursuing dreams and the Chinese dream of the rejuvenation of the nation.[53]

Thus, Xi has gone on to emphasize the unity aspect of the rejuvenation of the nation and his position towards Taiwan is definitely part of this great Unity platform that he is seeking to create with the greater Chinese civilisation and the ethnic Chinese people across the world. Here, there is even an attempt to appropriate both Confucius and the KMT's broader framework of nationalism. This is the discourse of 'Chinese exceptionalism', its enormous contribution to world culture in science and discovery and art etc. Quite different certainly from Mao, but not that different from Hu and the state support given to Confucian institutes. At the political messaging level, too greater use is being made of Sun Yat-sen as the representative of the leadership principle including the term *minzu* (nationality) instead of *renmin* (people).

Regaining lost territory is the final frontier and they have repeatedly identified these goal posts, Taiwan, the South China Seas and Arunachal Pradesh. "Territorality" is taking center stage in Xi's discourse of nationalism, linked as it is to the idea of national rejuvenation. Again, the use of history, especially anti-Japan rhetoric and the naming of the defeat of Japan at the end of the WW II Sept 30 as a national Martyrs Day and a holiday, are further indicators of their intent[54].

Finally, the key change that Xi has brought at the ideological and practical level is the re-centering of the Party that is being brought back as the leader of the nation. The Party as the uncontested leader and bringer of the transformation of China that all the others had failed to do. This re-centering is coupled with nationalism, creating what one clever researcher has called the Marxist mandate of heaven. The goal remains a *Xiaokang shehui*, again, a term actually in use by the intellectuals of

53. Xi Jinping (2107), *op.cit.*
54. Friso M.S. Stevens (2020), "China's long march to national rejuvenation: toward a Neo-Imperial order in East Asia?" *Asian Security*, 20 March https://www.tandfonline.com/ doi/full/10.1080/14799855.2020.1739651.

the 100 days reform in 1898, like Kang Youwei, who used the term to describe a society in the middle of transformation. Today it means a middle income country. The narrative now is one where the period of loss, subjugation and the century of humiliation approaches its end and China will claim its place as a *fuqiang guo*, a rich and powerful country.

Thus, Xi's China dream is both economic, a dream for a prosperous and largely middle class society and ideological as a dream of unity that celebrates the exceptionalism and greatness of China's culture and more importantly, the continuity that the CCP provides to maintain that exceptionalism with its socialism and market economy with Chinese characteristics. Only the CCP is capable of leading China to achieve its goals of greatness and truly rejuvenate the great Chinese nation.

The Chinese dream under Xi is of the unity of the great Han race and includes the territories populated by the Chinese such as Taiwan, Hongkong and even the overseas Chinese citizens of other countries who must per force share a love and admiration for the history of China.

In conclusion, one can argue that party discipline, party primacy and issues of governance that reinforce the leadership of the Communist party are amongst the chief narrative of Xi Jinping thought. Coupled with this is his concept of Datong or grand unity that includes all Chinese and the rejuvenation of the Chinese civilisation. This concept of *Datong* includes the territorial aspect and speak of uniting all the territories that China claims as its own. At the material level, the dream's goals are to build a prosperous society the middle of this century. The vagueness of the China dream also allows the government to continuously exhort the population to greater efforts to fulfill this dream.

Conclusion

Xi comes from a long line of Chinese leaders and intellectuals who have envisaged for China the long term goal of once again being a pre-eminent power in the world. Next year, as China celebrates 100 years since the founding of the Chinese Communist Party, China has decidedly come a long way since 1921, when its failed Republican revolution had plunged the country into a crisis of uncertainty about its future. Today China is a colossus and underestimating its resolve, sense of nationalist history and the personal determination of Xi Jinping to carve out his name in the annals of the Communist Party as the leader who took China to pre-eminent position in the world by uniting the country with Hongkong, Taiwan and those parts of India that it claims.

Xi has arrogated to himself all executive and political power. His anti-corruption drive and the constant hardening of his position where dissent and opposition to his policies and ideology is concerned, have created a situation of fear in China. The openness to foreign ideas is now systematically being curtailed and the teaching and dissemination of western thought, especially that of the Enlightenment period, with its emphasis on humanism and individual rights, democracy and intellectual criticism of Marxism is being severely restricted, with teachers of such courses being monitored by their own students just in case they teach something that goes against the narrow ideas of Marxism, now being pushed by Xi Jinping thought. Since his ascension, Xi has shown himself a leader capable of managing and controlling his party. He has also shown considerable skill and diplomacy in his own interactions with world leaders. He is generally regarded as a strong and courteous colleague. His country's economic clout and increasing leadership role in international institutions has further cemented the respect with which he is treated. In the end, there is no denying that Xi is a powerful and respected international leader. However, his totalitarian approach, both internally and externally, is not something that is going to be easy to pursue over a long term. It may actually be counterproductive to the goals of a **Fuqiang Guo** that continues to underpin the Chinese dream.

Chapter - II

Foreign Policy and the One Belt One Road Initiative

1. Foreign Policy Under Xi Jinping

Xi Jinping's ascendancy to power has been marked by visible changes in the foreign policy posture and actions of China. Under his regime, the concept of China's "core interests" (*hexin liyi*), has become clearly defined, along with its long term goals. These goals were already apparent during the time of his predecessor but their achievement has become a major aim of Xi's own goals for the nation. As Xi himself says:

> We will stick to the road of peaceful development, but will never give up our legitimate rights and will never sacrifice our national core interests. No country should presume that we will engage in trade involving our core interests or that we will swallow the 'bitter fruit' of harming our sovereignty, security or development interests.[1]

Xi Jinping is the first President and General Secretary of the Communist Party who has outlined a new Foreign Policy Doctrine by name. Called the *Xi Jinping Doctrine of Foreign Policy*, this has now become the basis for any articulation on foreign policy. Clarifying Xi's new doctrine, Fang Zheng points out the key reference points:

---

1. Xi Jinping (2013), 'Xi Jinping: genghao tongchou guonei guoji liangge daju, hangshi zou heping fazhan daolu de jichu' [Xi Jinping: to better manage domestic and international situations and to lay a solid foundation to the path of peaceful development], Jan. 2013, http://news.xinhuanet.com/politics/2013-01/29/c_11453 8253.htm.

> The surface-level frame of reference guiding this doctrine is "the mission of the Chinese Communist Party." In advancing this mission, Xi and the party draw on three deeper cognitive frames. The first of these—"national rejuvenation"—is focused on restoring China's wealth and power. The second and third deeper frames of reference—"global community" and "Chinese contribution"—aim to foster common interests and contribute to global governance.[2]

Culled from his various speeches, these foreign policy statements reflect once again Xi's prioritizing of the Party in the forefront. It is the aims of the Party that must define China's national interest and subsequently, international interests and here, under Xi, Reunification has become a major theme.

Reunification and Core Interests

From the time of Mao Zedong, claims to China's territorial integrity and unity have been paramount. This safeguarding and integrity of territory claimed by the Chinese, either based on traditional rights or history, has always been defined as China's core interests. And key to the concept of territorial integrity is National Reunification. This was clearly stated as far back as the 2011 White Paper on 'China's peaceful development'. This defined core interests in general terms as including 'state sovereignty, national security, territorial integrity and national reunification'.[3] China's Taiwan policy and its policies towards Tibet and Xinjiang, and other border regions, including Mongolia, must be seen in this light. Under Xi, this unity of Chinese territory and an expansion of its sovereignty over disputed territory has come center stage.

As Jing *et al* point out, over the years, China's definition of core interests has expanded to include new areas and new trade routes. The discussions and policy advice around how to effectively guard and restore China's core interests, is one of the key debates amongst China

2. Fang Zheng (2019), "The Xi Jinping Doctrine of China's International Relations", in National Bureau of Asian Research, July. https://www.nbr.org/publication/the-xi-jinping-doctrine-of-chinas-international-relations.
3. Jing Zhangshen, Yuefan Shao, Shaun Breslin, (2015) "Securing China's core interests: The state of the debate in China", *International Affairs*, 9 (12), pp. 245-266, March.

security specialists today. They point out that key thinkers and scholars are increasingly advocating a much stronger and overt policy towards all territorial disputes. The writers also point out that the US is identified as the key impediment to the fulfillment of China's ambitions.[4]

Jing *et al* highlight another important factor that is fuelling China's more aggressive foreign policy posture. This is the party led propaganda of nationalist recovery and the idea that only the CCP is capable of guarding and guaranteeing China's core interests and managing its rise. This is coupled with the idea that China is already a great power, raising national expectations of what China can and should do if faced with external threats. The idea of 'revenging' a 'century of humiliation', constantly taught in compulsory Patriotic learning Classes, adds to this nationalist oriented public sentiment.[5]

In this regards, "Wolf Warrior Diplomacy", is a phase one hears frequently in international media. This term, based on a Chinese lone warrior vigilante film[6] that was a super success in China, is meant to capture the sense of China's new aggression and power projections internationally. As Jian puts it:

> While Beijing still adheres to its declared 'peaceful development' policy aiming to maintain a stable external environment conducive to its ascendance, the manner in which it seeks to do so are considerably different from past decades[7].

So how exactly is Xi Jinping's foreign policy different from the past? Even some Chinese commentators have called the direction of Chinese foreign policy under Xi a new foreign policy, using the term 'New Diplomacy' (*waijiao xinzheng*) to describe China's foreign policy.[8]

During his report to the 19th National Party Congress of the Communist Party in October 2017, Xi could not have put it more clearly when he stated:

4. Jing et.al (2015), *ibid.*
5. Jing et.al (2015), *ibid*, p. 251.
6. Wolf Warrior is a 2015 Chinese vigilante film directed by Wu Jing. It showcases an Chinese action hero save overseas Chinese workers and property from mercenary Americans. See Alastair Iain Johnston, 'How new and assertive is China's new assertiveness?', *International Security* 37: 4, Autumn 2013, pp. 7-48.
7. Jian Zhang, "China's new foreign policy under Xi Jinping: towards 'Peaceful Rise 2.0", pp. 5-9, p. 5 Published online: 28 Jan 2015.
8. *Ibid.*

> The Chinese nation has stood up, grown rich and become strong – and it now embraces the brilliant prospects of rejuvenation.. It will be an era that sees China moving closer to center stage and making great contributions to mankind.[9]

Since then, Xi has been the face of Chinese foreign policy, leading from the front. The Center for Global Policy makes an assessment of the role played by Xi in public international diplomacy:

> Over the past five years, Xi hosted five major summits: the fourth summit of the Conference on Interaction and Confidence-Building Measures in Asia (May, 2014), the Asia-Pacific Economic Cooperation summit (November, 2014), the G20 Hangzhou summit (September, 2016), the Belt and Road Forum for International Cooperation (May, 2017), and the ninth BRICS summit (September, 2017). On top of these meetings, thirty heads of state and government gathered in Beijing on September 3, 2015, to view a special military parade that commemorated the seventieth anniversary of victory over Japan in World War II.[10]

This large scale attention to his role as a world leader is quite different from any past Chinese leader, except for Mao, who never really achieved the kind of acceptance, and even subservience, that Xi receives from Africa to Latin America. Xi truly strides large over the world and when he speaks, the world listens.

Differences with the Past

Two clear differences can be pointed out from foreign policy practices and discourse under Deng Xiaoping, one that emphasized China's Peaceful Rise and concentrated on expanding China's economic footprint. These differences are both ideological and practical.

At the ideological level, changes can be spotted in the discourse and writings of academicians and thinkers who have access to the leadership through membership of official think tanks. Here the advice of

9. Xi Speech at Party Congress.
10. Xie Tao, (2017), "Chinese Foreign Policy with Xi Jinping Characteristics", in Carnegie Tsinghua Center for Global Policy, Nov. 20 https://carnegietsinghua.org/2017/11/20/chinese-foreign-policy-with-xi-jinping-characteristics-pub-74765.

Deng Xioaping, "To hide one's strength and bide one's time", no longer finds adherents.

Yan Xuetong, the Dean of Qinghua University's Institute of International Relations and the editor of The Chinese Journal of International Politics, best represents this perspective. In 1996, Yan wrote **China's National Interest,** a book that reexamined China's national interest in a new light and emphasized China's need for new strategies to enforce this interest, including the exercise of multiple types of power, from economic and soft power to hard power. Yan Xietong best sums up this new real politik when he asks:

> "What is the point of having power if you are not going to exercise it".[11]

Such statements coming from one of China's more prominent foreign policy thinkers, is based on two assumptions. One, that China has the power and two, that it has the ability to exercise it. It is this open projection of Chinese power that has made the world sit up and assess China in a new light.

Scholars have stressed how Yan's book moved the debate on national interest away from a classical Marxist analysis by arguing that a distinction needs to be made between domestic politics where class interests may dominate and interests in International politics. The interests of the nation are the interests of the population as a whole and not representative of the interests of a ruling class[12]. Going on to define the understanding of National Interest in current China, Yong puts it aptly:

> China's recent conviction that international politics is now characterised by "the competition for comprehensive power" (*zonghe guoli de jiaoliang*) on a wide range of battlegrounds in,

11. Yan Xietong (1996), Zhongguo guojia liyi fenxi (Analysis of China's National Interests) (Tianjin: Tianjin remin chubanshe.
12. Yong Deng (1998), "The Chinese Conception of National Interests in International Relations", *The China Quarterly*, Jun., 1998, No. 154 (pp. 308-329, p. 313. Also see, Thomas Robinson and David Shambaugh (eds.), Chinese Foreign Policy: Theory and Practice (New York: Oxford University Press, 1993). See also Thomas W. Robinson, "Interdependence in China's foreign relations," in Samuel Kim (ed.), China and the World: Chinese Foreign Relations in the Post-Cold War Era (Boulder, CO: Westview Press, 1994); Thomas Christensen, "Chinese realpolitik," Foreign Affairs, Vol. 75, No. 5 (September/October 1996), pp. 37-50.

inter alia, military, political, economic and technological areas. Most Chinese analysts believe that, with the end of Cold War, "bloc politics" and ideological differences are less important; instead, national interests, especially economic interests, rise to pre-eminence.[13]

Thus, China no longer views the world as composed of competing class interests, defined by imperialism and the world divided into three large blocks of first, second and third world countries, the division of the world according to Mao, where China represented not just its own interest, but that of the Third World. Instead, it now locates its own place in international politics firmly within the domain of neo-realism, defined by an economic national interest that will create a peaceful environment. This emphasis on economic interest also forms the basis of Xi's One Belt One Road, that we shall discuss in greater detail.

These new articulations of foreign relations has led to claims that Xi has introduced new concepts into China's foreign policy. As Xue Tao puts them:

(1) a new type of major country relations, major country diplomacy with Chinese characteristics,
(2) a global community of common destiny,
(3) a new type of international relations[14].

In the first rubric, we must put Sino-US relations. The second includes Xi's neighbourhood and multilateral diplomacy, including his One Belt One Road and finally a new type of international relations literally means the end of the old order led by liberal democracies with a right to hold other countries to commonly accepted agendas on human rights, democracy, freedom of speech and other such norms. However, the key issue facing Xi Jinping is the Sino-US relationship as it transforms after almost fifty years of bonhomie and marked interdependence economically. This relationship will determine the other foreign policy strategies that Xi brings into play as China competes with the United States for influence in the world.

13. Yong Deng (1998), *ibid*, p. 315.
14. Xie Tao (2017), *op.cit.*

Sino-US Relations: A Rapidly Changing Dynamic

Xi, in his only speech to the Foreign Affairs community in the USA, had the following to say about a new type of Big Power Relationship:

> A number of things are particularly important for our efforts. First, we must read each other's strategic intentions correctly. Building a new model of major country relationship with the United States that features no confrontation, no conflicts, mutual respect and willing cooperation is the priority of China's foreign policy. We want to deepen mutual understanding with the US on each other's strategic orientation and development path. We want to see more understanding and trust; less estrangement and suspicion in order to avoid misunderstanding and miscalculation[15].

In the past five years, a lot has changed for Xi where his relationship with the USA is concerned. Today Xi's term as head of the government in China is more likely to be remembered as the one where a 'de-coupling and unraveling' of the Sino-US relationship has taken place. Despite claims to a great personal relationship with Xi Jinping, Trump has proceeded to launch a full scale trade and diplomatic war against China, a new addition to the existing pivot to Asia and the Trans Pacific Partnership that was launched by President Obama and subsequently, abrogated by Trump. While trade contradictions and tensions have existed even during the Obama regime, they have certainly come to a head under the Presidency of Donald Trump. These focus specially on the growing threat from China's unfair trade and diplomatic practices. Quoting from the US National Security Strategy of 2017, an article in Focus Asia points out that:

> These competitions require the United States to rethink the policies of the past two decades—policies based on the assumption that engagement with rivals and their inclusion in international institutions and global commerce would turn them into benign actors and trustworthy partners. For the most part, this premise turned out to be false.[16]

15. Xi Jinping Full Text from President Xi Jinping's Speech, given at a Dinner hosted by the National Committee on US-China Relations, in Seattle, USA Sept. 22, 2015 https://www.ncuscr.org/content/full-text-president-xi-jinpings-speech.
16. "Breaking the Mold: Trump's China Policy", Focus Asia Perspective and Analysis, Feb 2018 https://isdp.eu/content/uploads/2018/02/Trump-China-FA.pdf

Trump's America First Policy has targeted several countries but it is his targeting of China that has had the greatest consequences for both the USA and China.

Trump's main emphasis has been on the enormous trade deficit with China where the USA imports far more Chinese products than vice a versa. The following table provides a good overview of the history of US China trade and the increasing trade deficit between the two countries.

Exports of Goods, Imports of Goods, and Trade Deficit of the United States with China

Year	Exports	Imports	Trade deficit
1985	3,855.7	3,861.7	−6.0
1990	4,806.4	15,237.4	−10,431.0
1995	11,753.7	45,543.2	−3,789.5
2000	16,185.2	100,018.2	−83,833.0
2005	41,192.0	243,470.1	−202,278.1
2010	91,911.1	364,952.6	−273,041.6
2015	115,673.4	483,201.7	−367,328.3
2017	29,893.6	505,470.0	−375,576.4
2018	120,341.4	539,503.4	−419,162.0
2019 (Till March)	25,994.4	105,973.9	−79,979.5*

Source: United States Census Bureau, Foreign Trade, US International Trade Data.

The situation has not changed much since Biden has come to power. Instead, we see a bipartisan agenda where China is concerned. Biden and his team have continued to stress human rights and continued with sanctions against selected Chinese companies and individuals.

Thus, one sees a rapid increase in the deficit with China since the year 2000 and this has continued to rise during the years of Trump's Presidency. It is figures such as these that have allowed Trump to characterise China and Sino-US trade as unfair.

At the root of this conflict is the growing understanding in Western capitals that they have over the years enabled a regime that has consistently refused to democratize and play by international

* Usha Kashyap and Neha Bothra (2019), "Sino US Trade War" *Management and Economics Research Journal* 5 DOI: 10.18639/MERJ.2019.879180

rules of trade. The West's romantic belief that China's entry into the existing liberal and open international financial and trade order, would automatically force democratic political change in China, underlay previous attempts at engagement with China. The arguments for this, came to the forefront especially during debates concerning China's entry into the WTO.[17] Not only has this belief been systematically belied, instead China has become an economic giant, ready to challenge and change the terms of engagement with the world.

China must really be admired for its long term and comprehensive strategy to achieve its own goals of economic regeneration and military strength. It has systematically used all the international tools, institutions and treaties not just to integrate with the world but to ensure that the world is integrated with it. Further, it has done this on its own terms. While entering western markets as a member of the WTO, it has refused to follow suit where access to the Chinese market is concerned. Instead, its use of state funds to achieve a competitive edge for its products has allowed it to maintain a skewered balance of trade, leading to a general consensus that China uses unfair trade practices to maintain its edge in trade[18]. This lopsided trade relationship was partially tolerated as long as China remained a mere manufacturing giant, however, its sudden leap into the forefront of the information technology sector, especially cutting edge research and development in the fields of cyber technology and the internet of everything through 5G networks, has alarmed the Western world[19].

This alarm has been spearheaded by Donald Trump. Trump has not only castigated China from public forums but has also taken policy level action by imposing an additional tariff structure on specific Chinese products, forcing China to retaliate.

17. Belief of including China in international structures goes back to the beginning of US opening to China and accelerated after the economic reforms initiated by Deng Xiaoping. See Nicholas Lardy (2001), Issues in China's WTO accession", in Brookings, Testimony, Wednesday, May 9. https://www.brookings.edu/testimonies/ issues-in-chinas-wto-accession/
18. For a clear perspective of China's trade practices, see Michael Collins, "It time to stand up to China" in *Industry Week*, June 13, 2016. https://www.industryweek.com/the-economy/trade/article/21974236/it-is-time-to-stand-up-to-china
19. For a detailed and comprehensive analysis of China's growing dominance in future industries and informatics and the challenges facing its quest for global power, see Jonathan Fenby (2014) *Will China Dominate the 21st century*, Cambridge Polity Press.

Summing up this tit for tat, BBC reported that:

The US has imposed tariffs on more than $360bn (£268bn) of Chinese goods, and China has retaliated with tariffs on more than $110bn of US products. Washington delivered three rounds of tariffs in 2018, and a fourth one in September last year. The most recent round targeted Chinese imports, from meat to musical instruments, with a 15% duty. Beijing hit back with tariffs ranging from 5% to 25% on US goods.[20]

This was preceded by several rounds of trade talks that did not necessarily change the situation on the ground.[21] Studies show that both China and the USA have suffered economic losses due to this trade war[22]. Politically and economically, thus, recent contradictions and the emerging power struggle between China and the USA has become Xi Jinping's primary foreign policy challenge. This becomes even more important as we see a bilateral consensus amongst US political parties on the emerging China threat.[23]

Xi has already shown his complete disregard for international law and opinion by the unilateral abrogation of the treaty of Hong Kong that had guaranteed fifty years of autonomy to the city state. This, coupled with increased aggression and actions against Taiwan, is creating a real dilemma for the United States that has its own constitutional guarantees and acts of support if Taiwan comes under Chinese attack.[24]

Taiwan and its unification with China has been a Communist Party goal since 1949 and been at the center of tensions between

20. BBC, "A quick guide to the US-China trade war", 16 January 2020 https://www.bbc.com/news/business-45899310, accessed on 19 Sept, 2020.
21. Douglas Wong and Alain Chipman Koty (2020), "The US China Trade War: A Timeline", China Briefing, Dezan Shira and Associates, August 20, https://www.china-briefing.com/news/the-us-china-trade-war-a-timeline/
22. "China-US investment falls to lowest in almost a decade" *Financial Times* https://www.ft.com/content/458af94f-d152-47bf-8909-737f3ccce700
23. Hunter Dorwart (2020), "US Consensus view sees China as the Enemy", in *Asia Times*, May 22. https://asiatimes.com/2020/05/us-consensus-view-sees-china-as-the-enemy/
24. US guarantees to Taiwan in case of an attack by China are Constitutionally guaranteed under an exceptional defense partnership. Although the US is bound to come to the aid of Taiwan, there is nothing to say that it must put troops on the ground. For a detailed understanding of this partnership see, Richard Bush (2016). *The United States Security Partnership with Taiwan*, Brookings Institute https://www.brookings.edu/wp-content/uploads/2016/11/fp_20160713_taiwan_alliance.pdf

the United States and China since then. The USA had consistently supported Jiang Kaishek and Taiwan in the international community and allowed Taiwan to be a member of the United Nations and the Security Council. However, after the 1971-72 rapprochement between the two countries, the US summarily dumped Taiwan and accepted it as a part of China as part of the One China Policy. It is this framework that allowed Mao to sell the changed US China relationship to his own people and allowed China carteblanche into the world system. China's transformation into a world power is directly related to the early support and open policies adopted by the United States in the belief that the more China integrated into the world system, the more it would democratize and adopt international norms and institutions.[25] This major step laid the foundations for the new world order and China's increasingly assertive role in world politics.

From 1972 to 2020, the military and strategic capabilities of China have increased enormously, narrowing the gap between the USA and China and allowing China, for the first time, the comprehensive power to take on the USA if it was to use a military solution. Since his accession to power, Xi has openly espoused the use of military means to unify the country. This has become even more imperative for him as one of the goals and major achievements leading to 100 years of Communist Party Rule. Thus, Taiwan is a once again a crucial issue between China and the USA and could lead to military confrontation, if China does take military action against Taiwan, as more recent events seem to suggest.

The South China Seas and US Preeminence in South East Asia

Another rising area of conflict between China and the US, again with military implications, is the issue of China's claims to large parts of the South China Seas. China calls this as its Nine Dash Line that it identifies as its maritime borders. Currently, China has ongoing disputes with several ASEAN states such as Vietnam, Philippines, Malaysia, Japan, Brunei and Indonesia.[26]

25. US opening to China was one of the definitive changes in foreign policy since the second world war. See Henry Kissinger (2011), *On China*, Penguin Press.
26. For a brief but informative overview of the South China Disputes see Jihyun Kim (2015) "Territorial Disputes in the South China Sea: Implications for Security in Asia and Beyond" *Strategic Studies Quarterly* Vol. 9, No. 2 (SUMMER 2015), pp. 107-141.

While island building and land reclamation has been an ongoing project since Jiang Zemin's time, under Xi, this too has acquired urgency. During the past five years, China's infrastructure development and the building of defensive and offensive outposts in the region, has brought the USA and China once again into a direct confrontation since the USA has defence treaties with several of the countries impacted by Chinese claims.[27] Taiwan, Japan, South Korea all have strong defence treaties with the USA and also host US troops. Vietnam has recently moved closer to the US as a strategic partner and has been vociferous in its opposition to Chinese claims.[28]

Coupled with the increasing instability in the Taiwan Straits, the increasing competition with China in the South China Seas and the Pacific, attention has focused on China's increasingly efficient and powerful blue water navy. The latest data shows that China today has more ships than the United States and is rapidly acquiring ascendancy over the USA.[29]

Thus, the US-China competition for hegemony is playing out in multiple directions, especially in the fields of emerging information technology innovations such as 5G networks and in areas of cyber security. The USA's open war against the use of Huawei technology amongst its allies, and admonitions about China's cyber surveillance and data theft, has further raised tensions between the two countries.[30] More recently, the USA has taken to banning Chinese apps for sale such as China's WeChat and even TikTok Increasing decoupling between the USA and China has led Foreign Policy magazine to dub this The New Tech War. Pointing out how over the last three years, Donald Trump has

27. The USA's defense treaties in the East Asian region are discussed in detail in William Breer (2010), "US Alliances in East Asia: Internal Challenges and External Threats", Opinion Piece, May 12, BROOKINGS, https://www.brookings.edu/opinions/u-s-alliances-in-east-asia-internal-challenges-and-external-threats/
28. For the evolution of US Vietnam ties to the present, See Eleanor Albert (2019), "The Evolution of US-Vietnam ties", in Council on Foreign Relations, March 20 https://www.cfr.org/backgrounder/evolution-us-vietnam-ties.
29. For a comparison of the current state of the US and Chinese navies, see John Harper (2020), Eagle vs Dragon: How the US and Chinese navies stack up", in *National Defense*, 3/9/2020, https://www.nationaldefensemagazine.org/articles/2020/3/9/ eagle-vs-dragon-how-the-us-and-chinese-navies-stack-up.
30. The US China technology war is the emerging battle between the two largest economies. See Gordon G. Chang (2020), *The Great China US Tech War*, Encounter Broadside.

put in place the outlines of a policy on technology relations with China, Adam Segal says:

> That policy rests on restricting the flow of technology to China, restructuring global supply chains, and investing in emerging technologies at home. Even a new US administration is unlikely to stray from these fundamentals.[31]

It is keeping this new reality in mind that Xi Jinping has accorded special attention to developing self reliance in the field of technology and reducing its dependence on chip manufacturing from the USA. It has also reached out internationally to scientists with attractive deals to come work in China.[32] But over the years, we are bound to see a marked separation between the two technology regimes and their makers.

To counter American pressure and economic decoupling and what Chinese strategists have identified as "The contain China strategy", China has sought to formalise alliances and economic interaction through comprehensive trade deals, aid and infrastructure contracts and through security and strategic ties, Here Xi Jinping's signature One Belt One Road initiative is designed to play a major role. Not only is it being rolled out as part of China's common development goals for the neighbourhood but as China's contribution to world prosperity and advancement. Xi has invested his personal prestige and Chinese financial capabilities to further integrate the world within the Chinese project to compete as a big power. The One Belt One Road serves a dual strategic and economic sphere and is designed to replace the American presence in East Asia and Europe. It has already replaced erstwhile Russian (Soviet) domination in Central Asia. Not only does this project circle the globe, but it also lays bare China's strategy to dominate the world and safeguard its own trade and geopolitical alliances and interests. In the next section, we provide a brief overview of this project.

---

31. Adam Segal (2020), "The Coming Tech Cold War with China", in *Foreign Affairs*, Sept, October, Sep 20 https://www.foreignaffairs.com/articles/north-america/2020-09-09/coming-tech-cold-war-china.
32. Jun Mai and Amanda Lee (2019), "Xi Jinping calls for self reliance as China grapples with long term US challenge of trade war and ban on Huawei and other technology manufactures", *SCMP*, May 22 https://www.scmp.com/news/china/politics/article/3011388/xi-jinping-calls-self-reliance-china-grapples-long-term-us

FOREIGN POLICY PART II

ONE BELT ONE ROAD: CHINA'S NEW STRATEGIC AND TRADE POLICY

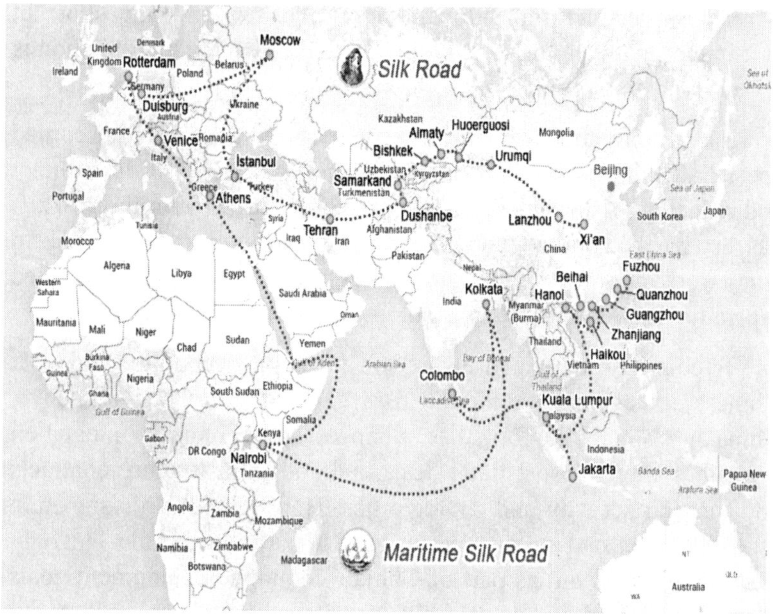

One Belt, One Road the name being given to Xi Jinping's personal initiative and thus, China's new strategic and trade policy, has long been in the making. It should be seen as the direct result of the long term forward planning that has existed from the time of Mao. The goal of Mao, Deng, and now Xi has always been the same, viz to enable China to once again 'claim its historical leadership role in the world'. Mao exported world revolution and claimed leadership of Asia and the Third World, a category he coined. In Asia, he challenged Nehru's and India's democratic traditions and institutions and, amongst the Communist countries and Communist parties, challenged Khrushchev after the death of Stalin. The quest being a strong sense of its own place in the comity of nations.

Deng Xiaoping changed the dynamic of China's interaction with the world by positioning China as a market economy and by participating whole heartedly in all 'free world' institutions such as the World Trade Organisation, ASEAN etc. If Mao took the socialist bloc and its ideology as his field of challenge. Deng turned to the leading power in the world, the USA to learn about how to become a great power, and finally today, reach the position to challenge its authority.

Deng has followed the model of building trade dependencies and now, aid dependencies with smaller countries, especially since the fall of the USSR in 1991. Deng's role lay in disarming the world and building bridges across continents. He built on the expectations of the US state and capital to integrate the huge Chinese market and to sell to this large country. He welcomed their investments and their technology. He encouraged 'sheathing the iron hand' and building one's strength or to quote him, "hide one's brilliance, don't take leadership but do some things (*taoguangyanghui, budangtou, yousuozuowei*).[33] His goal of a strong, modern China, an eminent China, goes back to the early twentieth century when learning from the West was seen as a necessity for China's own defence and rise. This is exactly what China did in the last two decades of the 20th century.

Goals and Imperatives

Several scholarly articles, conferences, policy statements and of course, Xi Jinping and Li Keqiang's personal endorsements, have clearly announced China's land and maritime Silk Routes as the blueprint for their future foreign policy, strategic and trade arrangements. Xi Jinping first spoke of his project during his address at Kazakhastan University in Sept. 2013, then in the Indonesian Parliament in October 2013 and this march in Baao[34]. Xi proposed three 'togethers:

-- discussion among the parties concerned to identify projects of cooperation and mutual benefit.
-- working together to realise the projects on the basis of common interest.
-- enjoying the benefits together from the fruits of this common endeavour.

---

33. Deng Xiaoping's speech during his Southern Tour in 1991, quoted in David Shambugh (2014), *China Goes Global: The Partial Power*, Oxford University Press, Oxford, p. 9.
34. Mandy Zuo and Kwang Man-ki, 'Xi Jinping Outlines an Ambitious Plan', in *South China Morning Post*, in http://www.scmp.com/news/china/politics http:// www. scmp.com/news/china/politics-policy/article/1749433/chinese-president-xi-jinping-promotes-regional-vision.

Speaking of these three goals, Wu Jiamin says they mean that China is not looking for unilateral gains but working the common prosperity since China's prosperity is inseparable from the world and the world's prosperity is inseparable from China's.[35]

China is today the largest trading partner of many countries and the trade in minerals and agricultural commodities such as soya are largely affected by what happens to the Chinese economy. Thus, one reason for China's aggressive trade networking is certainly the economic security it hopes to derive from the better integration of regional markets.

China provides several reasons for its new emphasis on multilateral trade and financial arrangements. It argues that multi-polarity is the general trend that will lead to peace and development and to ensure a stable financial world order and avoid the financial crisis of the past century.[36] Secondly, China has always shown great sensitivity to what it calls the USA's 'Pivot to Asia or Contain China', strategy and what was under President Obama, the US led Trans Pacific Partnership that was supposed to be the new trade alliance in Asia. China feels the interdependence of China's economy with those of different regions, and its global reach can and must be leveraged to counter any strategic or economic encirclement and secure China's status as a global economic and strategic power. It has already shown determination by putting together enough financial backing through its new Asia Infrastructure Investment Bank that has already seen participation by Britain, Australia and the Netherlands, despite a USA veto. Chinese scholars regularly argue how the recent international financial crisis has made it imperative that more equitable sources of financing are accompanied by a restructuring of international financial

35. Wu Jiamin quoted in "One Belt One Road", in *China Daily*, Jan 1, 2015 http://www.chinadaily.com.cn/china/2015-01/13/content_19309666. Also see, China's One Belt One Road, in Caixin online, http://english.caixin.com/2014-12-10/100761304.html

36. South China Morning Post Editorial, "One Belt One Road Initiative will Define China's Role in the World", *South China Morning Post*, http://www.scmp.com/comment/insight-Also see Wendell Minnicks, 'China's One Belt One Road Strategy' in Defense News http://www.defensenews.com/story/defense/2015/04/11/taiwan-china-one-belt-one-road-strategy/25353561/ Defense Newshttp://www.defensenews.com/story/defense/2015/04/11/taiwan-china-one-belt-one-road-strategy/25353561/

organisations. They also argue that trade interdependencies will make war costly.[37]

At the domestic level too, China hopes these development routes will help create greater wealth for its people as it leverages its financial capability and its labour power to win contracts. Trade linkages and joint financial investment in infrastructure projects will also allow China to expand its strategic interests, in the name of protecting its trade interests and its overseas workers. The greatest impact of this strategic outreach will be felt in the IOR region as China stresses its investment and links with the African Continent and in Central Asia as it reaches across by land and rail to Europe.

At the strategic level, the One Belt One Route was originally designed to counter the US led TPP (Trans Pacific Partnership) free trade agreement that is gathering momentum. This agreement has conspicuously kept China out. Despite Trump's pulling out of this treaty, China has continued with its own strategic intent. Thus, both strategically and economically China feels that the USA is trying to encircle and undermine its rise and China must find means to ensure and consolidate its economic and strategic interests.

Administrative Structure

To implement this policy and strategy, China has already put in place a comprehensive financial and organisational structure, from an Infrastructure fund of 40 billion and agreements signed with more than 26 countries in the region, connecting Africa with Asia and Europe. China's financial press claims that in 2015 1/4th or 26% that is 236 billion dollars is traded with Silk Route countries.[38] The Blueprint laid out by the Chinese government envisages seamless trade and cooperation at the tax, financial and trade policy levels. This sounds again like a common prosperity sphere or to use Xi Jinping's words, 'Community of Common Destiny', with the Beijing Consensus coming to fruition.[39]

---

37. Scott Kennedy and David Parker, 'Building China's One Belt One Road', Center for Strategic and International Studies http://csis.org/publication/building-chinas-one-belt-one-road
38. Figures in Xinhua Finance, 24-07-2015.
39. Xi Jinping quoted in Mandy Zuo in *op.cit.*

An official Ministry of Foreign Affairs Website puts it as:

> The connectivity projects of the initiative will help align and coordinate the development strategies for the countries along the belt and Road and tap market potential in this region, promote investment and consumption, create demands and job opportunities, enhance people to people and cultural exchanges.[40]

In terms of policy, a multilevel, intra-governmental macro policy has been devised like a single window clearance for projects related to this region and 12 central agencies have been assigned to this project. Five cooperative priorities have been identified: (a) policy coordination, (b) facilities connectivity that deals with international passageways, infrastructure networks, IT highways etc. Unimpeded trade through the removal of trade barriers, opening up of free trade zones, rationalisation of tax and customs structures and investment regulations, (c) financial integration both through the use of already existing cooperative associations such as SCO/ASEAN/ASEM/CASCF/China-Gulf, China –SAARC etc and the building of new financial organisations that deal specifically with the needs of this project. Finally, (d) there is greater emphasis on people to people exchanges with China emerging as an education hub in the region and Africa. This proposes to set up a Silk Route Tourism Infrastructure.[41]

As China's Foreign Minister put it:

> Our key focus will be making all-round progress in the "Belt and Road" initiative. We will further enhance policy communication with other countries, expand the convergence of our shared interests, and explore effective avenues of win-win cooperation. The emphasis will be on promoting infrastructural connectivity, and building overland economic corridors and pillars of maritime cooperation. We will also promote people-to-people and cultural exchanges and cooperation, and speed up relevant FTA negotiations. We are confident that the "Belt and Road" initiative will win even more support and deliver even more "early harvests", so as to catalyze the revitalisation of the Eurasian continent as a whole.[42]

---

40. Ministry of Foreign Affairs, March 5, 2015.
41. David Shambaugh (2014), in China Goes Global, *op.cit.*
42. Yan Xietong (2010), 'China' s foreign Diplomacy Should Reflect its World No.2 Status, in Guoji Luntan Bao Global Diplomacy, quoted in David Shambaugh, *op.cit.* p. 33.

Apart from these five cooperative agendas as keystones of regional foreign policy, Six regional zones have also been identified where China hopes its One Belt One Road initiative will emerge successful.

1. Europe: Is the end point of the land route. China hopes to become a strong technological partner and ultimately challenge the EU's dependence on the USA.
2. Central Asia: This is now China's backyard and it has replaced Russia as the primary power. Here China will be the aid giver and provide the funds for the development of largely Chinese SEZ's.
3. Middle East: This is part of China's energy security strategy and important also as a market.
4. East Asia: This regions trade and manufacturing is already closely integrated with China's and also where most of China's territorial disputes lie. This region is critical also because of the security and defense pacts that they have with the USA.
5. Africa: Has today become both a market, a source of raw material and a major investment destination for China. China has invested heavily in infrastructure development here and sees the defense of its trade routes to and from Africa as its right and justification for its naval presence in the Indian Ocean.
6. South Asia: In this region, China has expended maximum investment and diplomatic energy in its Pakistan relationship. Today too the port of Gawadaar and rail and road linkages being developed through the Gilgit, Baltisan region via the Kunjareb pass is designed to link finally through Iran to Turkey and Europe. Sri Lanka and the Maldives are already a part of China's maritime route and China had invested both in Hanbantota and Colombo under the Rajapakse government. India and Bangladesh are part of the BCIM that has already been officially signed by all concerned governments.[43]

Implications and Analysis

The Implications of China's new foreign policy are far reaching

43. David Shambugh (2014), *op.cit.*

and pose a challenge not just for the region covered by these routes, but for the international community as a whole. China, is in many ways, giving the world a fait accompli, telling the world that it has arrived and the world can either join it or then be left behind as China rises to claim its legitimate place in the sun. This is reflective of the foreign policy debates within China today. The slogans of Peaceful Rise and Harmonious Development have been shelved for a more aggressive foreign policy. They have been criticized for giving the impression that China will not challenge the status quo or push for greater power itself. They challenge the necessity to 'hide one's light'. As Yan Xietong puts it:

> Military, economics, culture are all sources of power. Without being used, they have no influence on others. Just as a military that is not used, is not a military.[44]

Part of the school of those identified as realists in China, these scholars argue that it is time for China to exercise its comprehensive national power and work more clearly to secure China's own national interest and security. This group according to Shambaugh, is also anti-western and filled with a sense of avenging past humiliations.[45] In fact, on most major territorial disputes, China has been taking a much harder line and has gone ahead with all its infrastructure development in the South China Seas, including its recent naval exercises with blatant disregard to how Japan, the USA or other South East Asian countries react.

China's One Belt One Road, is thus, a direct expression of this new line of thinking that is currently dominant in China. It is a consolidation of China's increasing power and a message, especially to the USA, that its role in South East Asia and South Asia and the Middle East will be contested and its institutional leadership in the economies of the region will be challenged. In the past we have often heard of the G2 emerging as a solution to the simmering conflicts in the Pacific and statements and denials from the USA and China on this arrangement. Today, the USA and China find themselves confronting real tensions in the South China Seas and the USA's pivot to Asia policy reinforced China's idea that the primary goal

44. Yan Xietong (2010), *op.cit.*
45. David Shambugh (2014), *op.cit.*

of US policy was the 'containment of China' and the further strengthening of its Asian alliances, especially with Japan and now Vietnam. Xi Jinping's One Belt One Route is designed to circumvent any such policy.

Since Xi has put his full personal weight behind this policy, we can expect it to succeed from the Chinese side. However, China will have to deal sensitively with issues of equality, sovereignty and people's nationalist feelings. It will have to up its soft power, something that it is singularly not doing, especially in the South China Seas. Its maritime going to be easy for it since it will directly challenge several regional powers and more importantly, the USA. However, its land route, cutting across Central Asia and into Europe has far greater chance of success especially since it already has a good working relationship with Russia and leads the SCO. Its AIIB Bank which now has a membership from New Zealand to England and the BRICS countries, is poised to challenge the World Bank and the IMF and will become the lead infrastructure lending bank in the region as more funds pour in from member countries. How China manage issues of independence and equality will determine the overall impact of its ambitious plans.

For India, the challenges of this strategy are complex as China definitely stakes its right to the Indian Ocean through its port investments in the neighbourhood. We have three options. One, to join the Quadrilateral of Japan, the USA, Australia and India and turn that also into an economic unit against the Chinese One Belt One Road. Two, build our own ports and trade ways on a war footing. We should immediately link Nepal, Arunachal, Bhutan and Ladakh through land highways and rail routes. Further strengthen maritime ties with Sri Lanka, Maldives, Bangladesh and our outreach capacities through the Andaman and Nicobar islands. Finally, India should take advantage of both if possible. Join the maritime leg of American alliances and the land route leg of One Belt One Road while building strong strategic alliances across the region and augmenting its own military modernisation. The South Asian and the Indian Ocean region is changing irrevocably. How India understands and positions its own long term interests is going to require bipartisan political consensus and cooperation.

Chapter - III

Theorising BRICS and its Cooperative Agendas

Introduction

Several questions naturally arise with regard to the growing institutionalisation of BRICS. These questions are being asked both within the member countries of BRICS and within the international community. The rest of the world largely views this group as, either lacking in substance or, as an attempt to project emerging economies as a power bloc that challenges the post 1944 world order. BRICS countries, rightly feel that their growing economic clout as markets and manufacturing hubs, means that they should have greater say in the global economic architecture. It is also seen as a group dominated by China, that has 75% of the BRICS GDP. This perspective is specifically true of American analysts who have commented on the purpose of BRICS as a grouping. However, though the member countries, and its political leadership are seen as enthusiastic, they themselves need to further clarify and put in place concrete mechanisms that further the goals of cooperation amongst them. In order to do that we need to spell out what BRICS means more clearly.

The first part of this paper hopes to discuss the following questions that the author has been grappling with in her own research. The first is, the nature of BRICS cooperation by briefly examining what scholars within and outside member countries are saying about this grouping, both in terms of public media coverage and in terms of policy statements. In other words, how is BRICS being theorised as a space for possibly coordinated policies and actions in the international arena? What exactly are the aims of BRICS countries vis-a-vis cooperative engagement and to what extent does 'national interest' compromise or promote a multilateral agenda amongst BRICS countries?

The second part of this paper will put forward areas where cooperative behaviour and agendas can converge. Although, a level of institutionalisation, headed by the MEA's of each country has evolved due to the annual Heads of State Summit, in the official Heads of State pronouncements, only intent is spelt out. Here we see a definite agreement on changing the economic decision-making order of the world and allowing emerging economies more say in international monetary and trade policies. BRICS member countries all agree that their rising and increasingly globalising economies means that they also have greater direct interest in the decision-making processes of international trade and finance. Thus, a basic common agenda has been repeatedly stressed at each summit. Little talk of any strategic or military cooperation has emerged.

Theorising BRICS

Theorising BRICS means, first and foremost, drawing upon definitions of multilateralism within International Relations theory and seeing how and if it applies to BRICS. Common goals, principles and institutionalised frameworks are often the hallmarks of multilateral fora. Within IR theory, it is argued that calls for multilateral action in the post Cold War world are the result of a shift in the balance of power, especially economically. The emerging economies are demanding more say in setting the global agenda as their own economies rise. Again, emerging economies see the benefit of working together to further their agenda for a more equitable distribution of decision-making at the international level.

Multilateralism in an institutionalised form, as different from alliances of the past, has been part of the global agenda since the end of the First World War when the League of Nations was set up. The limits of this early cooperation amongst European powers suffered largely because it remained a Eurocentric world agenda, dominated by colonialism where the rest of the world was concerned. The creation of the United Nations also coincided with the end of colonial domination and the emergence of several new independent countries in the 20th century. This in turn allowed the United Nations to emerge as a significant space of multilateral cooperation. The Cold War, however, ensured that the two super-powers divided the world into two camps and this division found itself reflected in the resolutions of the United Nations. It is only after the end of thc Cold War that we have seen the possibility of genuine multilateral cooperation amongst nations. This cooperation has been regional and economic, as in the case of ASEAN, NAFTA and political and economic as is the case of the European Union. Multilateral Cooperation has also taken on specific issue based on cooperative actions such as on Climate Change and Human Rights. This form of cooperation has been dominated by the NGO sector and these have acted as effective pressure groups on state led multilateral cooperation. This is evident in the case of Climate Change.

The coming together of BRICS countries can be understood using Robert Keohane and Joseph Nye's frameworks for understanding the new global order.[1] Their revised work continues to focus on the continuing role of the state in pushing foreign policy despite the emergence of non-state actors such as multinationals, NGO's and democratic politics. This perspective is valid especially for BRICS, where right from the beginning, a framework of multilateral cooperation has been State led and institutionalised through 'heads of state' summits. Expanding on Keohane arguments, Caporaso has argued that multilateral cooperation is based on three principles that distinguish this form from others. He names them as 'indivisibility, generalised principles of conduct and diffuse reciprocity.

By indivisibility can be thought of as the scope (both geographic and function) over which costs and benefits are spread, generalised principles of conduct usually come in the form of norms exhorting general if not universal modes of relating to other states. Diffuse reciprocity emphasizes that actors expect to benefit in the long run and over many issues rather than every time on every issue.[2]

This sharing of interest, where the benefits of each common action may not always accrue equally but may differ from issue to issue, has been

1. Robert O. Keohane and Joseph Nye (1998), "Power and Interdependence in the Information Age", *Foreign Affairs* Sept/Oct, 77/5 pg. 81 also see Keohane and Nye, *Power and Interdependence*, 1977 Longman.
2. Caporaso, James A. (1993), "International Relations Theory and Multilateralism: The Search for Foundations", in Ruggie, John Gerard (ed.) *Multilateralism Matters: The Theory and Praxis of an Institutional Form*, Columbia University Press, pp. 51-90.

the hall mark of why countries continue to engage in such cooperation. The coming together of BRICS countries while adhering to this principle, is different from other multilateral groupings in that it is not a regionally contiguous group and nor is it one based on economic or free trade agreements. Jim O'Neil, the Goldman Sachs researcher who first coined the word, had merely grouped the countries together under the category of Emerging Economies. The first initiative to push this group into a more binding and cohesive entity was made by Russian Prime Minister Primakov, who invited Brazil to become part of the already informal grouping of Russia, India and China. RIC, thus became BRIC and now BRICS, after South Africa too became a member. First held in 2009 in Yektarinburg, Russia, the Heads of States meeting of BRICS countries has gathered traction and become an annual event, closely watched by the world.

Several reasons have been attributed to the coming together of BRICS amongst western scholars. Many arguments give the BRICS grouping a largely economic and not a strategic agenda, arguing that continuing economic growth within a rapidly globalised regime is the main raison d'etre for this grouping. The Economist put it clearly when in a lead article it stated that BRIC (S) matter because they are large economies.[3] Four of the five countries in this group are trillion dollar economies. Other scholars have echoed this view point, pointing out that much of the BRICS rhetoric is hype generated to encourage investment and trade.[4] Scholars, such as Pape, have pointed out the 'soft balancing power' of BRICS countries, that is designed to counter the unilateralism exhibited by the United States after the collapse of the Soviet Union. According to Pape, it is the asymmetry of international relations that has forced middle power countries to come together.[5] Andrew Hurrell , echoes this perspective and points out that soft balancing "does form a very important element of the policies of Russian, India, Brazil and China. Hurrell is not speaking

3. "The BRICS: The Trillion Dollar Club", *The Economist*, April 15, 2010.
4. Skak, Mette (2011), "The BRIC Powers as Actors in World Affairs: Soft Balancing or.." Paper presented at IPSA-ECPR Joint Conference, hosted by the Brazilian Political Science Association, University of Sao Paolo, Feb 16-19.
5. Pape, Robert A. (2005), "Soft Balancing Against the United States", in *International Security*, Vol. 30, no. 1, pp. 7-45.

specifically of emerging economies, but what he calls 'revisionist states' when he says:

> Recognition and respect have been equally central to the demands of revisionist states...They have come more often from those states or peoples with the capacity to and political organisation to demand a revision of the established order and of its dominant norms in ways that reflected their own interests, concerns and values. Thus, a central theme of 20th century international history was the struggle of revisionist states for gleichberechtigung involving the redistribution of regional spheres of influence and the drive for equality of status within international institutions both formal and informal.[6]

Thus, the nineties that saw the collapse of a bipolar world also created the space for the emergence of a more balanced and shared decision-making structure in the world. This period also coincided with the rise of new economies such as the Asian economies of China, India and ASEAN. Latin America, with Argentina and Brazil leading the pack, also showed stable economic growth. All these countries were willing to reach out to each other in order to check the unilateralism exhibited by the USA, especially in Iraq. Russia and China, too benefited by alliances to check the USA.

Views from the United States point out that the rise of BRICS is certainly going to push for a redistribution of power within the international system and argue that the United States will have to follow the progress of BRICS countries as a group seriously in the future. In a previous paper, I have argued that that the United States is concerned both with maintaining the status quo and with trying to work within an obviously changing international order as BRICS countries start working jointly on a set of agenda based issues.[7]

---

6. Hurrell, Andrew (2007), On Global Order, Oxford University Press, London etc. pp. 45. Also see Hurrel, (2006), "Hegemony, liberalism and global order: What space for would be Great Powers?" in *International Security*, Vol. 30, no. 1. pp. 1-19.
7. Michael R. Brawley (2007), "Building Blocks or a BRIC Wall: Fitting U.S. Foreign Policy to the Shifting Distribution of Power", in *Asian Perspective*, vol. 13, No. 4, pp. 151-175. Also see, Thakur, Ravni, "The Relevance of BRICS', paper presented at the BRICS Think Tank meeting, Beijing, March 2011.

Other scholars have argued that there is no real common agenda amongst the BRICS countries and that contradictions between Russia and China and China and India will ensure that this grouping remains largely a paper tiger, especially with regard to concerted political action in the international arena[8](8). The contradictions and competition between India and China is often highlighted in this regard and attention has been drawn to divergent international goals, amongst BRICS countries. At this level, we see greater cooperation between Russia and China than amongst the combined five. This was clearly visible over responses to the situation in Syria and Libya.

A recent article in the New York Times too highlighted the lack of substance amongst BRICS countries. As Walter Ladwig said, "Aside from impressive economic growth over the past decade and an individual desire for a greater say in the institutions of global governance, these countries have little in common."[9] The range of debates shows that BRICS is being taken seriously despite the obvious differences within and amongst these countries.

Within BRICS countries, the role of China and its intentions has naturally generated the maximum interest. It is the largest economy and the largest trading partner of most countries in the world. It is also seen as the only real challenge to US supremacy. Alistair Ian Johnston, for example, studies whether participation in multilateral diplomatic institutions has helped reshape Chinese attitudes and approaches or whether China is engaged only at the level of tactical learning about how to manipulate regional institutions and not in altering or redefining fundamental interests. His extensive historical study of Chinese statecraft has the following to say:

> The perceived lessons of thousands of years of Chinese statecraft teach that multi-polarity is both unstable and morally illegitimate in a system that includes Chinese civilisation – the natural and inevitable state of which is to exist as the moral and political hub of the world".[10]

8. Walter Ladwig, "An artificial Bloc built on a Catch Phrase", in *New York Times,* March 29, 2012.
9. *Ibid.*
10. Alistair A Johnston (1995), *Cultural Realism. Strategic Culture and Grand Strategy in Chinese History*, Princeton University Press, also see Johnston and Paul Evans, "China's engagement with Multilateral Institutions", in

Thus, the world as such does not seem to attach too much importance to BRICS and scholars have instead sought to highlight the differences and individual goals of each country. This in fact means that BRICS countries will have to do more if they are to really engage each other in concrete agendas. However, it must be stressed that BRICS countries too have never emphasized on a concerted security or strategic agenda. They too have tried to focus on reform of international institutions rather than a confrontation with these.

Views from within BRICS

> BRICS is a platform for dialogue and cooperation amongst countries that represent 43% of the world's population for the promotion of peace, security and development in a multi polar, interdependent and increasingly complex globalising world. Coming as we do from Asia, Africa, Europe and Latin America, the transcontinental dimension of our interaction adds to its value and significance.[11]

This paragraph from the joint statement from The Heads of State summit, reflects upon how BRICS countries envisage their cooperation. Here the emphasis remains on the importance of multi-polarity within an increasingly interdependent world. BRICS emphasizes its transcontinental character as the key stone for a new paradigm of engagement, one that passes over geo-civilisational or regional contiguity as its main criteria.

However, within BRICS countries too, greater attention is being paid to BRICS issues. As pointed out earlier, this remains largely a state led initiative and its goals are clearly reflected in the joint declarations at each summit. The fourth summit held in Delhi, has once again highlighted main areas of convergence amongst these disparate countries. The point repeated through all the declarations, starting in Yekatenburg in 2009, is the common desire to open up global financial and economic institutions and give emerging economies more say in the international financial architecture in keeping with their global economic contribution. All the emerging economies have weathered

Johnston and Ross, *Engaging China: The Management of an Emerging Power*, Routledge, 1999, pp. 244-53.

11. *Delhi Declaration*: Fourth BRICS Summit, March 29, 2012.

the economic crisis reasonably as well as compared to G8 economies. This focus on economy is clearly brought out by the fact that points 6-12 deal with the international economic crisis and advocate the role that BRICS countries can play in improving the economic choices before these economies. To summarize from the leaders statements over the four summits held so far, the following points of common interest can be identified:

- Restructuring the financial and security architecture of the world
- Emerging economies must have more say in the decision-making bodies such as IMF and World Bank etc.
- Cooperation on Climate Change where the onus of funding rests with the developed world
- Strengthen multilateral organisations such as UN and not carry out international actions in a unilateral fashion.[12]

These four key points have appeared constantly in all the declarations while each summit has seen new additions to cooperative engagements in different industrial and trade sectors. Each government has also pledged support for greater academic and youth exchanges. Thus, a concerted effort is on to create greater awareness about the culture, politics and economies of the five countries. This soft power engagement can lead to interesting shifts in the way we conceptualise power sharing and international relations.

Within the academia and public media, the rise of India and China and Brazil has been theorised as a shift in power, and displacement of the center away from the West towards Asia and Latin America. Scholars in Brazil, where the Dependency theory of Immanuel Wallerstein and Andre Gunder Frank, still holds a lot of traction, both economic and political economy arguments are used to validate this inevitable shift of power. The rise of the periphery after five hundred years, or the end of the Vasco da Gama period[13]. BRICS as a group has also had a major positive development in terms of encouraging mutual research. Brazil has taken the lead here by institutionalising a BRICS Policy Research

12. Delhi Declaration: Fourth BRICS Summit, March 29, 2012.
13. Based on authors interviews conducted with various intellectuals/journalists in Rio de Janeiro, January 2012. Especially, Prof. Theodanis dos Santos and J Mauricio Dominguez.

Institute in Rio de Janeiro which welcomes researchers from BRICS countries. Each country now has scholars looking at common issues of climate change, social inequality, common problems of urbanisation and in identifying common international issues such as more say in the economic decision-making institutions of the world. Representative scholars from the concerned countries are now being introduced to each other and are discussed with interest. In Brazil, I found work being done on Amartya Sen and several studies on comparisons between India and China. Sen's cause of ethics in development, for example, is seen as an alternative model of development.[14] There is also a new pride and confidence in that Brazil has been chosen as the country that will provide the engine of growth in Latin America. An association with BRICS allows it to emerge as the gate way to Latin America and central to emerging power discourse in a multi polar, multilateral world order. This is the same feeling amongst policy-makers and thinkers in South Africa who point out the advantages that South Africa offers as a gateway to the African continent. For all countries, it is an interesting validation of their own regional importance and the fact that Indonesia and Mexico are keen to join in, proves that this is a prestigious gathering.

While Dependency theory and a shift in the balance of power may be the theoretical rationale for BRICS and what it represents in Brazil, India and China seek common ground by using the discourse of the 'Rise of Asia' and offset it against their joint experience and histories as ancient civilisations turned into colonised spaces, reclaiming once again their rightful place in the world. Having a shared colonial experience and a shared past, both countries have used the forum to emphasise their cultural commonalities and minimize differences. Intellectuals in both countries emphasize the virtues of multilateralism against unilateralism and some even place it higher than bilateralism. As Juan Deyang says, "Multilateral Diplomacy is more rewarding in finding and formulating solutions to global challenges which are transnational in nature".[15] Indian intellectuals like Prem Shankar Jha

14. Jose Maricio Dominguez (2006), "Amartya Sen, freedom and development: A critical view', in Sergio Costa et al (eds.) *Plurality and Modernity: De-centering Sociology*, Bande, Rainer Hampp Verlag, Munchen, Mering, 2006 pp. 179-194.
15. Juan Deyang (2011), "When is Multilateral Diplomacy more rewarding than bilateral Diplomacy" in *Reflective Diplomat*, March 7.

echo this praise for BRICS when, while commenting on the Delhi Summit, he says:

> Today BRICS has become far more than an acronym. The Delhi declaration contains not only the most comprehensive criticism of the failures of the West that has been voiced by any group of countries since the end of the Cold War, but also the outlines on an alternative blueprint for managing an interdependent world.[16]

The BRICS forum has emerged as an annual forum where Indian and Chinese Heads of State can meet for quiet bilateral talks. Working together in multilateral forums is seen as an important means of overcoming bilateral issues to work in cooperation on other issues. This also helps put in place the right atmospherics amongst the two neighbours. At the public media level, there is increased interest in the BRICS countries and more national media space is being devoted to the BRICS summit. Thus, overall, it can be argued that BRICS is definitely emerging as an important grouping of countries and has the potential to further strengthen its engagements.

Institutionalisation and the Way Forward

Like the idea of BRICS countries coming together in a group, the idea for further institutionalising the cooperative agenda amongst BRICS countries has also been pushed by Russia. Russian delegates at pre-BRICS summit think tank meetings have raised this issue during the China and the Delhi summit.[17] Russia strongly feels that institutionalisation, especially at the Secretariat level will lend BRICS resolutions and actions greater depth and also serve to consolidate opinion within BRICS. Not all BRICS countries have responded enthusiastically to this suggestion, preferring to go step by step. While Russian scholars argue for setting up a BRICS permanent Secretariat, a demand that is being discussed actively, BRICS has managed to institutionalise multilateral high level exchanges at

---

16. Prem Shanker Jha, "Delhi could be a Turning Point", *The Hindu*, April 10, 2012.
17. See the presentations of A. Vinogradov, "BRICS Dialogue Format and its Role in Formation of Multi-polarity", New Delhi Think Tank Summit conference papers, March 2012. This has also been discussed by other Russian scholars at the Beijing Think Tank Summit.

sector levels. BRICS trade, for example, has increased substantially and today stands at 230 billion dollars. The Delhi summit has seen greater progress made on this front, especially in once again setting up State led multilateral forums in trade, agriculture and the health sectors.

The new idea that has been favourably viewed by all parties is the setting up of a South -South Development Bank, an idea that was mooted and approved during the recent Delhi Summit. Although a long term project, this BRICS development Bank makes its intentions clear as far as the global economic architecture is concerned. BRICS countries are willing to come together to provide collective humanitarian assistance and fund infrastructural development in each other's countries. This is an important step forward for the BRICS countries to really emerge as the lead countries amongst the emerging economies and leverage their own economic growth and strengths to invest and trade amongst themselves.

At the analytical level, any institutionalisation process can be divided into two sometimes interlinked and sometimes separate mechanisms. These are:

(i) Economic and Track II levels and

(ii) Strategic cooperation at the international agenda.

This paper argues that any institutionalisation should first concern itself with cooperation within the economic and track II domains before raising expectations of cooperation in the international strategic sphere. If we look at the economies of the countries involved in BRICS, we see the possibility of greater engagement at almost every level. As the data in the graphs below shows, BRICS have a larger GDP than the G6 and future prognosis shows a constantly rising share of trade and GDP going to BRICS countries.

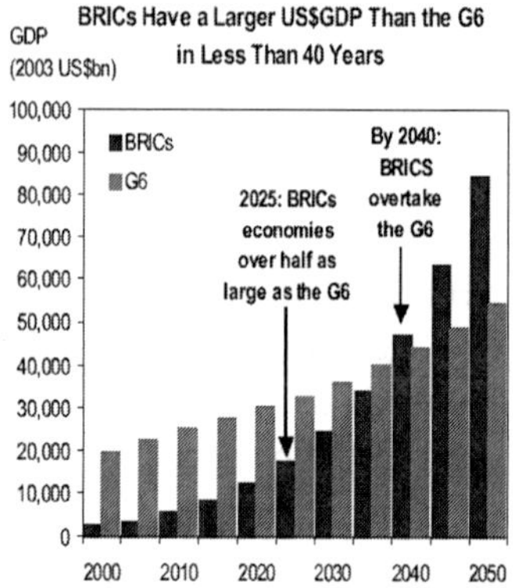
BRICs Have a Larger US$GDP Than the G6
in Less Than 40 Years
GDP
(2003 US$bn)
100,000
90,000
80,000
70,000
60,000
50,000
40,000
30,000
20,000
10,000
0
BRICs
G6
2025: BRICs economies over half as large as the G6
By 2040: BRICS overtake the G6
2000
2010
2020
2030
2040
2050

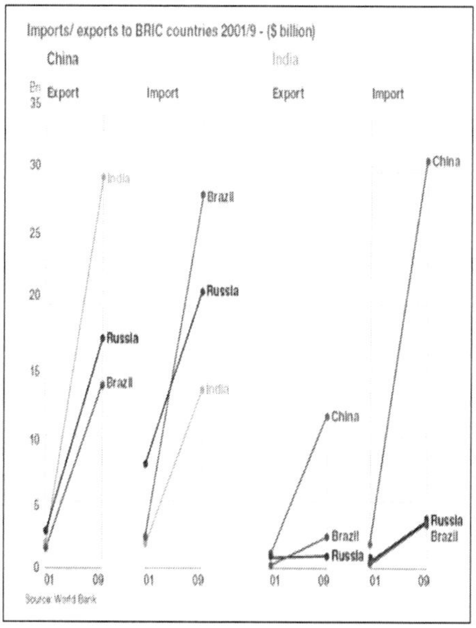
Imports/ exports to BRIC countries 2001/9 - ($ billion)
China
India
Export
Import
Export
Import
35
30
25
20
15
10
5
0
India
Russia
Brazil
Brazil
Russia
India
China
China
Brazil
Russia
Russia
Brazil
01
09
Source: World Bank

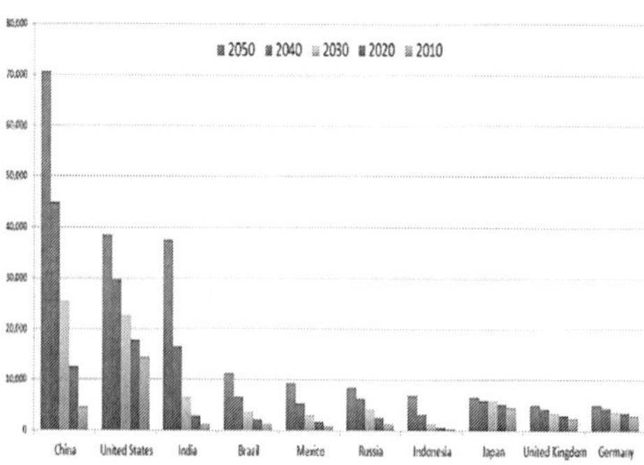
2050
2040
2030
2020
2010
China
United States
India
Brazil
Mexico
Russia
Indonesia
Japan
United Kingdom
Germany

It is at the economic levels that real traction and common interests can be identified. Thus, Russia's massive oil reserves can help augment the needs of China and India, both oil dependent countries. India can leverage its Information Technology and Service Sector, Brazil its agriculture and South Africa its minerals. However, issues of trade imbalances between India and China, as shown in slide 3, mean that greater efforts will have to be made through institutionalised mechanisms for all countries to achieve a genuine sense of 'diffuse reciprocity', as discussed in the beginning of this article. Ultimately, each country will have to perceive gain in this cooperation, if not on one issue, then at least in another. This is most possible where trade and economic exchanges are concerned.

At the security and strategic levels, several extraneous issues weigh in, making mutual accord more complicated. One of the more important issues remains each individual countries bilateral ties with the rest of the world and where India and China are concerned, a continuing trust deficit due to their boundary dispute. Although the Delhi Summit did make a joint statement on the recent Syrian and Iran issues, the statement itself did not go beyond emphasizing the need for dialogue to best solve the situation.[18] Within the United Nations, while voting on a Security Council resolution, we found the IBSA block voting together and supporting the efforts of the Peace Mission sent by the Arab League, while Russia and China opposed any intervention.

Another issue that can give rise to differences, where common security and strategic issues are concerned, is perception of this group being an anti-American or anti-Western group. Although the leaders of the respective countries have denied any such intent, often the impression given out is that this is an anti-western, anti-US group. Any talk of a strategic convergence would in fact be translated as such. This perspective again differs amongst the member countries, with Russia and China showing greater cooperation within the international arena than the IBSA block. This can, in turn, detract from the attempt of BRICS countries to find alternative solutions to international problems.

Bilateral issues and domestic politics within democratic countries can also create setbacks for any convergence on strategic issues. This

18. BRICS Heads of State, Delhi Declaration, *op.cit.*

is especially true for India and China as we have witnessed in the past where both Indian and Chinese media indulged in damaging rhetoric.

Thus, BRICS countries should first concentrate on creating a good working economic and trade relationship amongst each other and even within the G20 rather that wasting energy in attempting to create any institutionalised security architecture. Emphasis must, in the near future remain on track II, academic and trade exchanges to ensure that unnecessary friction does not arise.

India and China in BRICS

One of the significant achievements of BRICS has been its ability to get India and China to become members of this group. The credit for this must be given to Russia, that first mooted the ideas of a BRICS gathering. China and India within BRICS is a major gesture towards increasing interaction and cooperation between these two countries that have had a history of past conflict. However, despite their joint efforts within BRICS, the continuing trust deficit between India and China, means that especially on strategic issues, the two countries have distinct positions as already mentioned above. This is visible even where the common demand for an restructuring of international organisations such as the Security Council is concerned. Within BRICS, China is the only country that has not endorsed India's active pursuit of a permanent Security Council Seat. Similarly, China has not supported India's new nuclear status, endorsed as it is by the NSG. The two countries also have a different agenda where regional issues, a continuing border problem, that has in recent years, actually led to serious misapprehension within both countries.

One could, thus, argue that while India and China cooperate within a broad and rather superficial international agenda, the state of their bilateral ties will continue to influence their willingness to cooperate at a more substantive level. Nevertheless, the annual high level meeting between the two heads of state on the sidelines of BRICS summits, provides an opportunity for the two countries to engage with each other in a conducive atmosphere and creates greater avenues for trust. This growing engagement in multi-lateral forums is also reflected in their improved bilateral ties. Looking for common positions within multilateral forums can become an important tool for strengthening confidence and trust in bilateral ties as well. Thus, an expanding agenda for BRICS can also expand the cooperative agenda amongst China and India.

The BRICS Bank: Institutionalising Financial Cooperation

The start of the BRICS Bank has helped create the first state to state institution amongst the BRICS countries. The establishment of the BRICS New Development Bank, first mooted by India, and formalised during the 2014 summit held in Fortaleza, Brazil, became a reality in July 2015. From the very beginning, BRICS has stated economic cooperation and especially the need for the emerging economies to have a greater say in the international financial and international economic decision-making structures, as its main goals. Emerging economies felt disadvantaged by the status quo and proceeded to take common positions within the G20, yielding rich dividends.

This sense of comprehensive economic cooperation has been clearly visible since the first Joint Statement of the BRICS country leaders at the first summit held in 2009 in Yekaterinburg in Russia, where as states earlier, leaders put forward their commitment to advance the reform of international financial institutions so as to reflect changes in the global economy. The emerging and developing economies must have a greater voice and representation in international financial institutions. BRICS's Common Economic Strength BRICS as a combined economic unit makes up 20% of global output and its share according to Forbes has risen four fold in the past decade. However, although their economies have slowed, in light of the international economic crisis, they still represent strong fundamentals. It is these strong fundamentals that the BRICS countries bring together in the institutionalisation of the BRICS New Development Bank. BRICS countries have outlined an agenda for financial and investment cooperation through its combined financial contributions. The key focus here will be infrastructure and clean energy investments.

China is certainly the largest economy in this combination, making up 70% of the BRICS combined GDP. It is also the host of the Bank, with headquarters located in Shanghai, naturally making Chinese staff and infrastructure locally responsible for the smooth functioning and logistics of the bank. While all countries will share in the layout of initial capital with fifty billion each, China will be the largest funder of the CRA or contingent reserve arrangement. China will contribute 41 billion USD to this fund, Russia, Brazil and India will contribute 18 billion each and South Africa will come in with 5 billion. India has the first rotating Presidency, under K.V. Kamath and will be followed by Brazil. South Africa has won the right to host the first regional headquarters. In 2016, the BRICS bank has already disbursed loans to member countries as a handout by the Bank shows below. We notice that the key focus of the banks loans has been in the clean energy sectors and here we have seen a lot of movement of cooperation between the BRICS countries, with Climate change top of the agenda for sustainable project funding and sustainable economic development. At the same time, President Kamath has stressed the need to make projects profitable and capable of returning the loans disbursed. The BRICS bank is not meant to be a charity but a professional bank that uses professional and international criteria for its functioning, thus increasing its cooperation with other international financial institutions.

Thus, right from the start BRICS has started functioning as an effective mechanism for timely and needed support for energy efficient clean technology projects and has sought to invest in infrastructure upgrades in this sector.

Pending Issues: The Nature of Mutual Trade

The key issue that will remain in terms of effective economic financial cooperation between the BRICS countries is the issue of trade imbalances and today, the declining imports to China, of raw materials from BRICS partner countries like Brazil and South Africa. This has already registered a negative impact on their economies. These countries are seen as large resource delivering bases for China's ever expanding market. Russia is a source of cheap energy for the same market while providing a large market for cheaply manufactured Chinese goods, something that India, for example, has seen to the detriment of its own manufacturing sector, apart from other internal policy reasons of course. China also runs a trade deficit in its favour with all these partner countries. China's economy is larger than that of the four other BRICS economies combined. China's exports and its official foreign exchange reserves are more than twice as large as those of the other BRICS economies. Thus, China makes up 70% of the BRICS economic heft. Without China, BRICS loses considerable stature.

It is this fundamental dominance of China, both in its reach and its capacities that should prompt a little wariness on the part of its other member states. Is the bank going to become another Chinese bank like the Asia Infrastructure Investment Bank, where China is again the lead partner? Only the USA and Japan have stayed out. This will certainly give competition to the Asian Development Bank, with Japan as a key shareholder. Some have argued that China will also gain by hiding its investments in Latin America and Africa through the BRICS and AIIB rather than being targeted for its huge investments directly. The Chinese yuan has already been accepted as one of the international reserve currencies, thus lending in Yuan through the BRICS bank will further enhance the Yuans status as an international currency. China, thus, seems to be the net gainer in the BRICS bank, although countries like India will benefit by having another source of government borrowing outside of the IMF and the World Bank.

At the geo-political and internal economy level, the smaller IBSA group of India, Brazil and South Africa, that also exits has a lot more in common than with Russia and China that are emerging more and more as a common block within the Security Council and on other international issues. India, with its own needs of greater and broader cooperation with the USA, a move quite visible under the Modi government, may find itself in a difficult position within BRICS on several strategic and economic issues.

To what extent a common Bank leads to greater international synergy and who is the largest beneficiary of this new grouping, will remain the key questions for these BRICS partner countries. While a need to restructure international institutions, including the Security Council is felt in common, these are not acceptable to all our partner countries. India, for example, despite BRICS, is still hedging with regard to China's other economic initiatives such as the One Belt One Road project. Nor can Brazil and South Africa be part of this project, based as it is on contiguity of trade and infrastructure routes. However, if the BRICS economic cooperation leverages the fundamental comparative advantages Expert Opinion- BRICS Economic Cooperation 12 of each country than there is a chance of future and long term success. This means, Brazil with its resources and its high tech industry, Russia with its high technology and its cheap energy sources, China with a qualified manufacturing labour force and its huge wealth, India with its IT source strength and human capital and South Africa with its resources should work together to leverage and maximize their strengths while learning from the best practices in technology and planning. The world does need a more equitable distribution of power and the emerging economies, including Russia are right to ask for this but this should based on practicing what we preach, first within our own group.

Conclusion

The Heads of State Summit of BRICS countries in 2020 will be the 12th such meeting, proving that a process that began tentatively, has today garnered synergy and moved forward enough to put in process the idea of a BRICS Bank. The continued support provided for the idea of a BRICS group of countries from within these countries, and the special role being played by the States of each country in keeping the momentum going, ensures that BRICS as a group of countries willing to work together is here to stay. This group does represent the principle of diffused reciprocity as stated by Keohane since it is not based on direct or even simple national interest. It is difficult to argue what each country gains by this membership but easy to see how they all gain a greater speaking voice as a group. This is what makes BRICS interesting since it does not represent mere regional interest but actually seeks to create a group with inter-continental reach. Although Russia, India and China do share an Asian identity, the inclusion of Brazil and South Africa, gives this group a more international image.

While the demand for a more equitable economic architecture and institutions remains the first point on this common agenda, we are today seeing a process of growing institutionalisation taking place. Gains in trade and common bargaining on trade issues will definitely begin happening. To what extent, this group succeeds in evolving a common international agenda is something that remains to be seen. There is a confidence and sense, both of entitlement and right, that one witnesses when intellectuals in BRICS countries speak of how they envisage the world today and how they envisage a new post Cold War world order. All the countries involved within this grouping, with the exception perhaps of Russia, are countries that previously belonged to the third world and were colonised countries. The post nineties has thus witnessed the emergence of new countries with a different set of aspirations and a different framework for sharing world problems and decision making. In the final analysis, BRICS is a grouping of emerging economies who seek to provide an alternative agenda for handling this complex interdependent world. Their coming together also ensures that no one country can emerge as a unilateral power in the twentyfirst century and that cooperation and multilateral solutions are the way forward. This check on unilateralism may well be the biggest contribution of BRICS.

The changing international scenarios and the now emerging tensions between the USA and China may also impact the BRICS cooperation agenda in the future. However, they will have the instituionalisation and operationalisation of the BRICS Bank to their credit.

PART - II

EMERGING SOCIAL ISSUES

Chapter - IV

The Dynamics of Social Stratification in China

Introduction

> Mechanical and superficial views still boast empirical and ideological clarity, yet they invariably depend on obsolete binary opposites – state vs. society, official vs. unofficial, and dictatorship vs. democracy – Xu Dongzhang.[1]

China today represents a country that cannot be simply classified any more according to the old frameworks within which it was approached. Western scholars of China have always tended to understand China through the limited framework that Xu criticizes in the above statement. New forms of material power distribution, social representation and ideological contradictions are often ignored under the circumstances. China represents a complicated plurality dominated by a new socio-economic polity. China is not a unitary society but one that is beset with difference and contradictions that have huge implications for the future of China and its internal organisation. These differences, competing discourses, of legitimacy exist at different levels in the body politic of China.

Several changes since the 1980's and more markedly since the turn of the century, have today coalesced to create a new discursive reality of power and control in China. It is a well known fact that China since the economic reforms is today a highly stratified society. This has meant that instead of class solidarity, new discourses of nation building, loyalty, and a harmonious society are premised on a shared

1. Xu Dongzhang 2001, p. 2. *Whither China: Intellectual Politics in Contemporary China*, Duke University Press.

nationalism and ethnic homogeneity. The appeal to Confucianism and a Harmonious society, to the glories of the Ming Empire, hark back to this Han eminence. These changes are visible in different areas. First, the discourse within the Party, about its own role and ideology. The second is the role played by Education in China today towards cementing social stratification in China and finally if what we are seeing in China can be called a class. Is this socio-economic revolution in society leading to the reemergence of a capitalist class? Who does this consist of? Is there an identifiable capitalist class, middle class in China etc? However, this new discursive reality is not without contestation within China itself, within academia and within the Party.

To understand the repositioning of the Party at the ideological levels, and the debate that this is unleashing, it is intrinsic to understanding the different layers of social stratification, or to use Bourdieu, difference, distinctions, that one sees in China today. In this paper, we hope to move away from the stereotyping of Chinese society while at the same time attempting to grasp the seeds of contradiction that exist within Chinese society. Contradictions that if taken to their logical conclusion can undermine the stability of the country and force the Communist Party into a corner.

Ideological and Intellectual Level

The last few years have seen several books that have pointed out the internal problems that beset China today. Susan Shirk's book, *A Fragile Empire* is only one in a long list of such thesis's. The contention of my paper is that the comparative openness of Chinese society today, the rise of intellectual think tanks and their contacts with the West and above all the emergence of China as a class stratified society, has created inevitable contradictions with the ideology professed by the Communist Party. The first major change at the ideological level is within the Party itself. While the Communist Party is today trying to play a centralist role between the different strands of opinion that exist amongst the intellectual think tanks of China nevertheless, it has changed at all levels, throwing up new oppositions, reflecting these new dynamics of an increasingly stratified society. The Party too, since the 1990's has of course, changed radically in character and become a technocratic Party with younger and more qualified people. A 2008 article by Sato and Eto on "The Changing Structure of Communist Party Membership" points out how since the 1990's the Party has outlined four criteria or four transformations for Party membership. These are revolutionised (*geminghua)*, younger (*nianqing hua*) intellectual and well educated (*zhishi hua*) and professionalised (*zhuanye hua)*.[2] This change coincided with Jiang Zimin's agenda to make the Party more inclusive and broaden its reach to include those previously defined as class enemies. Thus, the Party has changed in both ideology and recruitment of cadre, resource/criteria for Party membership. This is both reflective of social tension and social stratification that is emerging in China. And here, education, socially stratified education is playing a fundamental role in turning this social stratification into a generational and regional, and like in every other place, becoming a purveyor of distinction, an issue that I will take up later in the paper.

Along with its criteria for membership, the Party took the lead in redefining the aim of China's development strategy from socialist modernisation to a socialist market economy. This emphasis on 'market economy' has created for the first time, serious contradictions at the intellectual level. The joke in China today is a pun on the word *qian* – which is the same for future and money even though the characters are different. *Xiang qian kan,* they say no longer means look to the future but look to money! This has further exacerbated the idea of Chinese society as a capitalist society led by a Communist Party that still supposedly rules in the name of the working class. A quick look at the distribution of membership among private entrepreneurs makes for interesting reading. Jie and Dickson differentiate between red capitalists, i.e. those who were already members of the Party and or ran SOE's before being classified as entrepreneurs and those who have joined the Party after being classified entrepreneurs. Out of the total of 2,048 members they interviewed, 8 percent are red capitalists the rest were those who became members after.

In field work that I carried out in China in 2006 amongst students of three prestigious universities, Chengdu, Yunnan and Beijing, I was told that membership of the party is crucial for serious upward

2. Sato and Eto, "The Changing Structure of Communist Party Membership", 2008, p. 654.

mobility and provided stability no matter what one did. Out of the 150 students I interviewed, every one had applied for membership and 64 were already members. The result of this changed recruitment criteria has meant, as I actually argue, that the Party as such has become middle class in nature just as higher education has. Educational criteria remain extremely important for membership. This middle-classing of the Party has provided the Party with broad support within urban China and amongst the educated elite. At the same time, it has delegitimised the Party amongst the very constituents it traditionally empowered, the peasants and the working classes. Amongst them, the Party is corrupt and capitalist. And field work shows that what we see is the emergence of what Solinger calls "cadre merchant", Y So, calls "embourgeoisement", others "state capitalism", "clientele capitalism", etc[3]. It is this merchant – bureaucrat embedded network that is today seen as the economic, political oppressor. This also means that anger against social conditions, corruption and emerging class contradictions in the capitalist industrial sector, are directed at the state. The state is not a mediator amongst class conflicts, against unfair authority, instead, it becomes the source of conflict. This is what is the first fault line in China today.

An emphasis on educational qualifications, automatically implies that a large population of workers and peasants who only make it through the compulsory nine years of education, and in rural areas, some not even that, automatically lose out on membership. I don't know how many have seen the film by the famous director Zhang Yimo called "Not one less". It is a documentary drama that speaks of the state of rural education and is the story of a village school that is left in the care of a young girl while the teacher goes on leave. She is left with the instruction to ensure no student goes missing. Access to education, especially higher education, is thus becoming a major point of social stratification. This will be discussed in Part II of my paper.

It is these redefinitions that have led to wide scale debate amongst the intelligentsia. The debate amongst them hinges on both development policy planning and on how far China should turn into

3. Solinger, D.J, "Urban Entrepreneurs and the State: The Merger of State and Society", (1992), Aurthur Rosenbaum (ed.) State and Society in China: The Consequences of Reform, Boulder Press, p. 36

a genuine market economy. This debate is couched both in terms of ideology and economic planning. The first, is part of the great reform economics that was led by Deng. These are ideologues who categorically support the reform process and staff the State's think tanks, especially under Jiang Zemin. The main thrust of this argument remains grounded in market economics, globalisation and also the decentralisation of economic planning. The second group, that can be described as university intellectuals, writers and members of civil society, are not opposed to reform but have launched an ideological attack from a New Left perspective. This group has concentrated on the negative fallout of the economic reform process by focusing on increasing economic disparity and social disparity in China. A second cleavage is the push for Liberal democracy both within the Party and amongst civil society.

The new left critique is represented by scholars such as Xu Dongzhang, Wang Hui and members of the Sociology departments and CASS departments. Here scholars like Li Peilin etc are the leading lights. They have collected extensive field work data documenting income and educational disparities in China today.

First the theoretical critique. Authors like Wang Hui who was editor of the journal *Dushu*, are critics of the process of globalisation and neo-liberal economic paradigms. Wang Hui puts this quite clearly when he says:

> China's continued support for socialism poses no obstacle to the following conclusion: In all its behaviours, including economic, political and cultural – even in government behaviour – China has completely conformed to the dictates of capital and activities of the market.[4]

It is the social processes unleashed by becoming a market economy and a capitalist state, albeit under the continued guise of a Socialist state, that motivates the ire of Wang Hui and other scholars. They go on to attack the commercialisation of society and the role of the contemporary Chinese state as a handmaiden of global capital. Their criticism is that Chinese intellectuals who have bought into

4. Wang Hui 2001: p. 161 in Xudong Zhang (ed). *Whither China: Intellectual Politics in Contemporary China, Op.cit.*

the ideology of globalisation have either turned to tradition such as Confucianism on the one hand, or have pushed the theory of the rise of Asian capitalism and China's important role in this rise. The mix of nationalist desire for super power status also comes in for criticism. Shaoguang Wang, for example, reiterates the role and necessity of the state, especially where welfare policies are concerned. Criticising those who advocate a deepening of the market economy and withdrawal of the State he argues that, "Some people believe that once the stifling state is knocked out of the economic realm, market forces would emerge full blown to put human society in perfect order". This he goes on to argue, is "the most dangerous of illusions".[5] Thus, we see that a strong theoretical new left critique of China's economic and global strategies. This critique is extended to all aspects of contemporary Chinese society, to the commercialisation of its culture, the rise of conservative politics and at traditional discourses that have reemerged after years of authoritarianism.

This critique of the growing inequalities in society has been further corroborated by excellent research carried out by social scientists in CAAS and in other departments of the Social Sciences. The 2005 Blue Book of Sociology, is an excellent example of the attention being paid to this issue. At the annual Chinese Sociology conference that I attend, I was able to meet a lot of the people working on such issues, including members of the New Left group that I spoke of. Wang Hui, for example, is quite a hero amongst students.

The 'discourse of democracy' in the party is also worth commenting on. In the post Tiananmen society, the demand for democracy does not come from society as a whole but from within the Party. A good example of this is the kind of curriculum and books available within Party schools which are attended by more than a several cadre on an average. Studies show that today the issue is not one of redness of class background but of standing by the Party's goals. This can be done by subscribing to China's economic modernisation but does not necessarily mean support for a single party state. There are people within the Party intelligentsia who believe that along with a liberal economy, a liberal democracy should also play a role in national politics. While the eighties saw a call for democracy within a Marxian

5. Wang Hui, 2001, pp. 207-08 (*ibid*).

paradigm, intellectuals like Su Shaozhi, Wang Ruoshui etc is a case in point. They asked for 'socialist democracy and legal rights for citizens, today it is people like Li Shenzhi, former Vice President of the Chinese Academy of Social Sciences and a former Vice Minister who is the leading voice of change. Feng Chongyi in a 2008 article, which I consider excellent, quotes Li as saying in a book in 1988:

> After three hundred years of comparison and selection in the whole world since the age of industrialisation, and particularly after one hundred years of Chinese experimentation, one of the largest in the scale of human history, there is sufficient evidence to prove that liberalism is the best human value.[6]

This is corroborated by my own interviews with students, those able to, and willing to, aspire to the middle class and middle class liberalism. This younger generation also saw middle class values as including multi plurality. Feng goes on to quote another senior Du Guang, former head of the Party School, who wrote a long article on party authoritarianism or communist despotism. This article, even went as far as to ask for the army to be separated from the Party, and grant independence to Unions such as the Trade Unions.

All these critiques are based, in my analysis on the fact that the ruling party is pursuing an ideologically contradictory agenda. For example, within the Party, the CCP has already set in place a more democratic agenda. The General Secretary does not get more than two terms, their response to Maoist totalitarianism and Deng's biggest contribution to democracy, is fixed terms for all members of leading bodies within the Party, the Prolitburo, the NPC etc. Xi Jinping, since coming to power in 2012, has changed this generally accepted term limits and as we move towards the Party conference at the end of this year, Xi will probably be reappointed as General Secretary for a Third Time.

Despite such moves within the Party, where the rest of the people are concerned, 'the aam adami of China', the Party remains authoritarian. The CCP and its allies internationally, like our own CCP remain caught in a time warp. They are competing with the

6. Fei Chongyi, "Democrats within the Chinese Communist Party since 1989, in Journal of Contemporary China, 17, (57), 2008, pp. 673-688 : 675.

internet, sms etc in terms of continuing to exercise control. They have a hundred thousand employees trawling the internet every day. Now here, the CCP is exhibiting features of totalitarian regimes that were not necessarily Marxist. It is today a totalitarian and rich capitalist party, which draws its support from a middle class and the class of private entrepreneurs. It also seeks its support, like capitalist totalitarian regimes across the world, from an embedded middle class and the beneficiaries of economic reform and above all total support of the People's Liberation Army. The Party stands as a representative of a Capitalist State. It is, not, today, the representatives of the working class, the peasantry or the hordes of migrant labour. This is a feeling that is common amongst the common person of China, and I have interviews with a cross-section of groups that corroborates this feeling. For them the Party now represents big business, corruption and a lack of concern for them. It is this general sense of disenchantment with the Party that has led Xi to prioritise his idea of Common Prosperity, and hit out at the private sector and the enormous inequalities in China.

Zhang Wanli's article in the special issue of the Social Science Academy looks closely at the way the market economy has influenced the social structure in China and resulted in changes in the allocation of resources. He characterises this change by three major elements:

(1) By the possession and redistribution of power.

(2) By the emergence of free flowing resources and free space outside the old system and

(3) By the evolution of social relationships from universalism (every one was comrades) to utility oriented relationships.[7]

He contends that the total capture of power relationship by the Communist party will no longer be the only one in the evolving social landscape although it will remain dominant. Here the emergence of a vibrant and free commodity exchange market will determine the relationships between various social groups. According to the three basic changes identified by him, Zhang lists five major interest groups within urban China today. Broadly, these are workers, peasants, cadres, intellectuals/white collar service sector and private business owners.

7. Zhang Wanli, "Twenty years of Research on Stratified Social Structure in Contemporary China", *Social Sciences in China*, Spring 2002, p. 49.

Thus, market reform and the greater freedom in terms of access to resources and decision-making is seen as the fundamental impetus for the emerging social differentiation in China.

Part II: The Dynamics of Social Stratification

At the theoretical level, the paper raises questions of how practices of social stratification and social inequalities can be identified and whether "Class", remains an appropriate mechanism for using as a criterion of social stratification. This issue has been well discussed by scholars like Kornai and Paulowski who have looked at post-Socialist societies in Eastern Europe. Kornai, for example, speaks of communist societies as creating vertical dependencies linked to a system of patronage represented by the party.

Sun Liping, speaking about China, hits the nail on the head when he points out that "The possession and redistribution of power relating to social resources characterised the pre-reform party structure of social interests".[8] Till the reforms, Chinese society, especially in terms of wealth, was hardly differentiated. Riskin, for example, points out that until 1981, the gini-coefficient was only 0.16, a very small amount. Other studies have pointed out that in terms of income differentiation, the span ranged from thirty to 560 yuan among government cadres and an official guideline set a ratio of 6:1 for top and bottom wages in all enterprises. Amongst the rural population, around 60 percent were classified as middle peasants.[9] Of course, the role played by privileged Party status, was out of the purview of classical definitions of inequality. Today the situation is radically different. In 2000 the gini coefficient stood at 0.458, clearly showing the stark inequalities that are beginning to exist.[10] These are of course, macro indicators of growing social income inequalities and point to a definitely emerging social stratification.

Today the road to upward social mobility is Education and the differences in educational attainment have become a basic root of

8. Sun Liping, "Reaccumulation of Resources: The Back-ground of Social Stratification in China in the 1990s" *Social Sciences in China Today*, Spring 2002, pp. 21-39.
9. C Riskin, "*China's Political Economy: The Quest for Development since 1949*", (Oxford, Oxford University Press, 1987), 89.
10. Sun Liping, "Relations, Social Relations and Social Structure", *Shehuixue Yanjiu*, 1996, no. 5.

social stratification. Deng Xiaoping put an end to the politicisation of education in China once he embarked on Economic reform. Educational policies, especially since the late eighties were designed to create an educated labour force that would fit into China's overall economic modernisation drive. The goal was to increase productivity and the pursuit of social mobility. As the Minister for Education said in a recently published book, "If China is to sustain its economic development and growth...education is the essential tool to help achieve this goal and transform its huge population into a resource".[11]

In China, the law gives each level of government its own educational jurisdiction. Education at the secondary school level and lower level is administered by the local people's government. Here access to resources and amenities is determined by two factors, regional both rural and urban inequalities and the private and public sectors. Overall, the central government has left the requirements of compulsory education to local levels. It has largely stopped funding this sector and the onus now lies on regional governments. In terms of percentage of percapita, Central government investment has never been more than 2.4 percent and this figure ranks China 114 in terms of nations. Basic education is thus the responsibility of the local government and so is the mobilisation of sources. Here again, several studies, such as that by Xuelan Rong show that poorer counties tend to spend less on this provision. As they point out one, third of educational funds come from provincial governments, one-third from local and poorer localities tend to allocate less funds. Thus, per capita expenditure per child can vary from 2,786 yuan per annum in richer east coast regions to 422 yuan in counties located in the western poor provinces of Guizhou or Gansu.

Education in China is no longer free and the cost of education is a major impediment to access. Here several studies prove that parental income is the main criteria for educational attainment. Here access to, allocation of resources and nature of establishment are private or state key schools or normal schools is essential. The quality of the teachers, the access to educational aids and the social capital enjoyed by different schools, thus varies widely. Once again, it is a myth that education in China is free. That is not the case since books and

11. Zhou Ji, 2005, *Higher Education in China*, Thomson Learing, Asia.

stationary has to be bought by the individuals. Similarly, payments are demanded for school buildings and sometimes, communities have to even pool in for teacher's salaries. The government is also encouraging foreign universities, private education at different levels and forcign funds to come in. They have also brought in community funding and asked industrial enterprises to help with this sector for special Today private school education has become a major criteria of both social and income upward mobility. Private education is certainly adding to growing stratification and the differences in the facilities provided. Private education must also be distinguished from another level, that of key schools. These are government run institutions where the goal of China has been concentration of resources. These key schools make up 20 percent of primary and elementary schools and get 80 percent of sources. They are called Zhangxin xiao xue. Thus, they get the best teachers, students, facilities and administrators. The competition here is fierce and Party membership, especially children of senior party cadres have a significant advantage. Private schools are expensive and like in India the preserve of the emerging rich in urban areas. Fees can vary from 5,000 yuan per annum to 21,000 yuan.

The basic divide and source of economic social inequality in China was the *Hukou* or residence system. This permit determined not just access to all the facilities available to an urban resident but also ensured the rural population remained confined to the country side. Education in these areas was limited to basic literacy or primary education. The three R's and this too varied by region. This area of Chinese education has suffered greatly in the post-reform era for two main reasons. First the changed financial structure, where the onus for primary and secondary education falls on counties and is in turn passed on to the lower village levels, especially for the primary areas. And secondly because of the large scale out migration of labour from these areas. Rural areas, must once again be determined by region and are symptomatic of the regional divide that is now overwhelming in China. The drop out rate from poorer regions after primary school can often be higher than fifty percent. One of the factors contributing to this phenomenon is the fact of out migration where a large number of children now live with grand parents who may in turn be literate or semi-literate. Basic salaries for uneducated unskilled labour, domestic and service based is 500-700 yuan per month.

All these different elements have contributed to the increasing social stratification in China today and are to a large extent a reflection of this aspect. Access to quality education at different levels is symptomatic of an increasingly diversified society. While earlier different kinds of state institutions and within them 'key schools' within the state sector provided 'quality education', membership of the Party was one of the main factors for access. Here of course the main and obvious divide is again between rural and urban areas and even more so between rich counties in the coastal region and poor counties in minority areas and in the interiors of Anhui, Jiangsu and Guizhou. Today access to education is closely tied to occupation, income and party membership. How are these status groups being defined and understood within China? And how is social stratification being analysed is the next question that arises. And finally, does the State at all have policy responses to this emerging stratification? The next section will corroborate my claims of China as an emerging class society where internal contradiction at the social and economic levels echo the concern and conflict that is visible at the intellectual levels.

The Blue Book of Sociology, (2002) lists ten major clearly identifiable 'status' groups.[12] The main article that looks at the different segments of society in China today is by Li Chunling and his team from the Social Science Academy. They identify ten major social segments that can be seen in China today.[13] At the theoretical level, one notices an absolute refusal to look at these social segments emerging as 'classes'. American sociology and differences in terms of income, education etc are prefaced rather that the term "class origin". And in a way, they are right because these groups still do not identify a cohesive class interest. I will deal with the use of class for these segments in a later section. However, right now, they are both fluid and not yet generational in nature. The groups are:

1. *State and Social Bureaucracy*: This group consists of party cadres and administrators at all social levels. They are seen as the group that pushes through the economic reforms and is still responsible for decision-making at all levels from the

12. *The Blue Book of Sociology*, (2002), Social Sciences Document Publishing House, Beijing.
13. Li Chunling & Chen Guangjin (2002), "Report on the Social Stratum and Structural Changes," in *Blue Book of Chinese Society*, (Beijing: Social Science Publishing House, 2002), pp. 115-132.

center to the county and village levels. They make up 2.1% of the total working population and in cities 1-5% and in rural areas 0.5%.[14] Li Qiang, for example, concludes that the major changes that have occurred in the profile of this section is three fold: (i) their number has increased, (ii) the average age has fallen and (iii) they have markedly better cultural and educational backgrounds.[15]

Other researchers have been looking at how the power originally allowed to this group by virtue of their total control over the distribution of sources has been affected by a market economy. Sun Liping (2002) points out that "In the transition towards market economy, the redistributioneers (the erstwhile power elite) cannot become rich by only relying on their political stock in trade."[16] In the past of course, becoming a party member was the only way to join the elite group. Today, however, one can become a member of the elite group through economic success. Thus, money is becoming a criteria for elite status.

2. *Economic Managers (jingli renyuan ceng)*: This class consists of both those who manage private enterprises and those who manage state enterprises. The origins of this section is three fold. First those who managed state or collective enterprises. The second, those who have emerged from the private sector and from technical and management trained backgrounds. They are responsible for introducing modern management techniques. The third group is financial consultants and managers.

   This is a largely urban based group and have high education and specialised backgrounds. This is an important and powerful section and stands at 1.5 percent of the urban working population.[17]

14. Li Chunling & Chen Guangjin (2002), "Report on the Social Stratum and Structural Changes," in *Blue Book of Chinese Society*, (Beijing: Social Science Publishing House, 2002), pp. 117.
15. Li Qiang (2002: 52), "New Changes in Social Stratification", in *Blue Book of Chinese Society*, Social Sciences Publishing House, Beijing 2002.
16. Sun Liping (2002), "Reaccumulation of Resources: The Background of Social Stratification in China in the 1990's," Social Sciences in China Today, spring, p. 36.
17. Li Chunling & Chen Guangjin (2002), "Report on the Social Stratum and Structural Changes," in *Blue Book of Chinese Society*, (Beijing: Social Science

3. *Private Enterpreneurs*: This is the newest group to emerge in China and owes its existences solely to the economic reforms. Li Chunling describes these entrepreneurs as those who employ more than eight people. Within the overall picture, this group forms only 0.6 percent of the population and the gap in numbers between economically vibrant areas and backward areas is high. 3 percent of their total numbers are in developed areas and 0.3 percent in underdeveloped areas.[18]

These entrepreneurs initially emerged in the rural areas and in townships. Because of the ideological limitations to their position, this group was initially slow to expand. In the beginning they were largely made up of urban youth returning to the cities after the Cultural Revolution, laid off workers and emerging rich peasants who had diversified into cash crops. Socially, they came from a low social background. After 1992, once the ideological limitation to their position had ceased, this group increased its social status and its economic clout. In the middle of the eighties, as Zhang points out, scholars were more interested in the "internal composition, class nature and group characteristics of this group.[19] Jia Ting and Wang Kaicheng (1989), two people I interviewed pointed out that although they hired labour, they could not be characterised as capitalist exploiters because they did not live entirely on interests. Today, of course, China has very successful private entrepreneurs and this group has become the main group able to expand both its social status and its economic power.[20]

Specialised Technical Personnel: This group consists of those involved in both private, joint ventures and state enterprises. They are an important group in China's drive towards modernisation and enjoy a high social status. They can also be seen as the modern intellectuals

---

Publishing House, 2002), p. 118.

18. Li Chunling & Chen Guangjin (2002), "Report on the Social Stratum and Structural Changes," in *Blue Book of Chinese Society*, (Beijing: Social Science Publishing House, 2002), p. 118.
19. Zhang Wanli, "Twenty years of Research on Stratified Social Structure in Contemporary China", *Social Sciences in China*, Spring 2002, p. 54.
20. Jia Ting and Wang Kaicheng (1989), Interview with Author, Ravni Thakur, Beijing, Sept 25, 1989.

as against traditional intellectuals.[21] However, their numbers make up only 5.1% of the total work force and the difference in rural and urban areas is huge. In urban areas they make upto 10-20 percent while in rural areas their numbers do not exceed between 1.5 – 3 percent.

White Collar or Middle Management workers: This section of white collar workers is seen as made up of non-technical staff in all enterprises and consists of 10-15 percent of the total labour force.[22] This is also the one sector through which workers and peasants can improve their status and provides the channel for upward social mobility. The numbers of these workers has increased since the reforms started.

Individual commercial and industrial workers: This section has also increased in number since the reforms and this sector has expanded since the eighties. Since the nineties the reform of state enterprises, a large population of erstwhile workers have entered this sector. This includes all kinds of services provided. They make up 4.2 percent of the urban labour force.[23]

Commercial Service Sector Workers: This sector has the greatest relationship to the urbanisation taking place in China and consists of all types of commercial and service enterprises. In most urban areas they make up to 13-17 percent of the working population. However, in the rural areas, this figure declines to 1.6-3 per cent. Thus, the contrast amongst rural and urban areas is strengthening, especially if we keep in mind that it is the service sector that is seen as the growth engine in both India and China.

Industrial Workers: This group is largely marked by a decline in its social status both at the ideological and the income levels. Amongst the ordinary workers, again there is a marked difference amongst those working in the private sector and those still employed by a shrinking

21. Li Chunling & Chen Guangjin (2002), "Report on the Social Stratum and Structural Changes," in *Blue Book of Chinese Society*, (Beijing: Social Science Publishing House, 2002), p. 119.
22. Li Chunling & Chen Guangjin (2002), "Report on the Social Stratum and Structural Changes," in *Blue Book of Chinese Society*, (Beijing: Social Science Publishing House, 2002), p. 119.
23. Li Chunling & Chen Guangjin (2002), "Report on the Social Stratum and Structural Changes," in *Blue Book of Chinese Society*, (Beijing: Social Science Publishing House, 2002), p. 120.

state sector. This difference translates into income, security and status. Zhang points out how during the reform of large and medium sized enterprises about 30 million workers have been made redundant. This makes up 30 percent of the total state labour force. Amongst these, the majority are women and middle-aged workers.[24] This sector makes up 22.6 percent of the total work force and within this, peasants now comprise 30 percent.[25] This is because several younger workers in this sector have improved their technical skills and moved into other professions.

Peasants: This group forms the group that has undergone the most remarkable stratification. The difference today amongst a rich peasant, middle peasant and the poor peasant who becomes a rural migrant are extreme today. The peasant can be further sub-divided into those engaged in fishery, animal husbandry and floriculture. The incomes of those involved in these commercial farms is much higher than those engaged in conventional farming. Li points out how the contribution being made to the national GDP has declined from 28.1% in 1978 to 17.3 % in 1999.

Unemployed, Laid Off workers and Part Time workers: This is naturally the lowest section within Chinese social strata at the moment. However, according to Li they make up only 3.1 percent of the total, a figure that seems disputable if we keep in mind the way the manufacturing sector in China operates today.

While the Blue Book of Sociology, published by Academy of Social Sciences lists these ten groups and one notices that this is because explicit divisions are made amongst the different sectors and workers belonging to these different sectors. However, the issue of the Social Sciences in China today adds another group. That of Intellectuals. Huang Ping divides intellectuals in modern China into three types: Those inside the system, those outside the system and those opposed to the system. Those inside the system are ones who helped in policy making, those outside were ordinary, academic intellectuals and finally the opposed formed the dissident groups that

24. Zhang Wanli, "Twenty years of Research on Stratified Social Structure in Contemporary China", *Social Sciences in China*, Spring 2002, p. 52.
25. Li Chunling & Chen Guangjin (2002), "Report on the Social Stratum and Structural Changes," in *Blue Book of Chinese Society*, (Beijing: Social Science Publishing House, 2002), p. 121.

we know suffered. Here intellectuals like Wang Hui et al would be classified as academic intellectuals.

Let us also briefly look at this stratification in terms of income. An extremely interesting and good article by Sun Liping examines this problem. Sun looks at the new methods through which resources were redistributed and the process of the re-accumulation of resources. He points out that during the eighties, this process was characterised by the emergence of what came to be known as *guandao* (bureaucratic profiteering). This helped a number of people possessing or having access to political and administrative power become rich. Some of them became the shiwan or ten thousand households and some went on to become well known entrepreneurs.[26] He points out that corruption and the use of government contacts remained a main source of wealth accumulation right through to the nineties and by the nineties the sums involved were in millions of yuan. However, in the nineties, the losers in the reform process started to show up. This is immediately visible in the income differentials of the noveaux riche and the marginalised poor.

Sun tells us that if we examine data showing the distribution of income of various social strata in China, we find that it is beginning to form a pyramid. According to him a survey by a researcher in the people's university in China showed that the share of income received by the highest fifth of household in total income is rather high. Especially in rural areas, the richest fifth received 48.9%, in urban areas their share accounted for 44.46 percent of total income. Classified as the intermediate strata, the household incomes were 15.01% for rural households and 15.77% in urban households, making it less than 20 percent of the whole.[27]

Yang Yiyong and Xin Xiaopai (2002) take a more detailed look at income differentials in China. The first major difference of course lies in rural and urban areas. Giving statistics from 1998 –2000, they show how rural incomes have been consistently lower.

	Urban	Rural
1998	5458	2162
1999	5888	2210
2000	6316	2253

26. Sun Liping, "Reaccumulation of Resources: The Back-ground of Social Stratification in China in the 1990s" *Social Sciences in China Today*, Spring 2002, p. 61.
27. Sun Liping, "Reaccumulation of Resources: The Back-ground of Social Stratification in China in the 1990s" *Social Sciences in China Today*, Spring 2002, p. 64.

The latest UNESCO figures also speak of increasing rural urban income gaps.

This data shows us that rural incomes are half that of urban incomes, although both are increasing. The article also goes on to give us income differentials amongst the different professional occupations. It notes that jobs in the financial sector, electronics and information industries, aviation and tourism, insurance etc have seen the largest increase in incomes in comparison to workers and peasants in traditional jobs. These are capital and technology driven industries. In contrast labour intensive industries have seen their incomes fall.[28] Differences amongst these different stratum are also visible in terms of income. As the following table shows:

The name of a social Stratum	Personal income (monthly)	Family income (monthly)
Leader in Institutions	2000	3,500
Office workers	1,376.4	2, 385
Professional and Technical personnel	1,368.8	2,683.2
Commercial workers	1,447.7	2,720.1
Labourers	998.0	1,845.5

(*Source:* Qiu Liping, (2002) "A study and Discussion of Social Strata in Chinese Cities Today – Taking Shanghai as an Example", in *Social Sciences in China*, Spring 2002, p. 73.)

Thus, in terms of income there is a marked difference between the different segments and allows us to clearly see the segments that can be classified as middle stratum. One also notes that most Chinese survey's concentrate on the different professional categories to specify social stratification. In this respect, the professional background of a person is likely to be the determining factor in terms of other forms of social and cultural capital.

This income differential is further corroborated by my research and also reveals the importance of "occupation" in determining status and wealth. In Chengdu, for example, the average middle class salary is considered between 3000-5000 yuan and above ten thousand yuan to qualify as upper class.

---

28. Yang yiyong and Xinxiaobai (2002), "Status and Trends in Income Distribution" in *Blue Book of Chinese Society*, (Beijing: Social Sciences Document Publishing House, 2002), p. 145.

The role of the Intermediate Strata or the Middle Class

Now the question that obviously arises is whether these different strata/groups, the language that the Chinese use, can at all be seen as classes or whether interest groups is all that they will remain. Also whether these groups actually have well articulated interests. A brief analysis of the data presented above and the way Chinese scholars are identifying separate interest groups, it is easy to see that despite the small number that are falling into the middle stratum, it is still significantly large in numbers to become a powerful segment. However, in the main, this segment consists of the 'salaried' classes, with rich entrepreneurs forming the uncertain top.

I was able to find only one article that deals directly with the emergence of this middle strata. This is by Xiaohong Zhou. Titled "The Middle Class: Is it possible and is it necessary." The article explores the rise of the middle class in China and attempts to theorise the issue. Using Marx, the author argues that the middle class is the inevitable result of industrialisation and in post-industrial societies, forms the majority.

As Zhou points out:

> Since the economic reforms of 1978, the class structure of Chinese society that had stabilised over the last thirty years again revealed a new change. One undeniable fact is the deepening and continuous impact Chinese economic reforms have made in changing China's social structure. Apart from the traditional working and peasant class, a new class has emerged. A new middle class stratum. This class which had disappeared from the historical stage after the success of the Chinese communist revolution since 1949, has not only once again reappeared, it has developed with a remarkable speed.[29]

A spokesman of the State Information center said "In the first five years after 2001, 200 million people will enter the group of middle stratum group".[30] And the deputy chief of the Foreign Trade Bureau

29. Zhou Xiaohong, "Zhongchan Jieji: Heyi keneng yu Heyi ke wei?" (The Middle Class, Is It Possible and Is It Necessary?), *Sociological Seminar,* Dept. of Sociology, Nanjing University, no. 15, Sept. 18, 2002, p. 1.
30. Zhou Xiaohong, "Zhongchan Jieji: Heyi keneng yu Heyi ke wei?" (The Middle Class, Is It Possible and Is It Necessary?), *Sociological Seminar,* Dept. of Sociology, Nanjing University, no. 15, Sept. 18, 2002, p. 1.

in a speech in Singapore during talks on China entering the world market was even bolder, in ten years time China will have 400-500 million people with middle level incomes.[31] However, there still remain certain ideological impediments, the Chinese state in official documents does not use the term "middle class", it only uses the terms, "middle income-stratum" or "middle-income group".

Zhou goes on to define this group as those who belong to the following:

Post 1978 new private entrepreneurs in cities and towns

Post 1978 private shop keepers and private manufacturers

Government bureaucrats and intellectuals

White collar employees in foreign companies

Managers in different sectors

High income groups in new industries, and students who have returned home from abroad and finally, sports and media stars, models, and artists.[32]

This division would also correspond with the first six categories listed by the Blue Book of Sociology. Thus, we see that there is a definite segment in China, which corresponds to what is accepted as the middle class world wide and is emerging as the consumer section of Chinese society and increasingly is being driven by consumption patterns whether of commodities, leisure, art etc. They are, to use Bourdieu's term, becoming 'distinctive' in life style. If one were to add up the percentages given by the Blue of Sociology in terms of the different strata, then the middle segment would form approximately 27.5 percent of the total working population. Thus, more than a quarter would fall in this bracket.

In analyzing the role that this stratum could play in terms of the emergence of a civil society, almost all the articles surveyed seem to be pessimistic. Here the continued control of the State and the Communist Party are seen as the major reasons. As Qiu points out,

> Although a market economy is necessary for a civil society, it does not necessarily lead to one...The unmatched and enormous

---

31. Zhou Xiaohong, "Zhongchan Jieji: Heyi keneng yu Heyi ke wei?" (The Middle Class, Is It Possible and Is It Necessary?), *Sociological Seminar,* Dept. of Sociology, Nanjing University, no. 15, Sept. 18, 2002, p. 2.
32. Zhou Xiaohong, *ibid.*

role played by state power makes the people increasingly exert themselves to seek individual power. Under these circumstances, it is less possible for us to establish a civil society of equality and autonomy".[33]

He goes on to say that "We believe it is hardly possible for China to form a middle class with an independent social stratum of entrepreneurs and intellectuals as its main body".[34]

Zhou sees their main role in China as the front line of consumers rather than as political actors. This role, he says is already prominent.[35] This consumerism has of course come under criticism and this class is dubbed as one "which spends tomorrow's money to manage today". Their political role he sees as that of a rear guard. Zhou puts it succinctly when he says:

> They are the group that has benefited the most since economic reforms. Had access to better education and white collar jobs. At another level they have contributed to social stability. Essentially they draw their status from their salaries and jobs. And depend on themselves to further improve their status.....Intellectuals and journalists from this segment have also tried to create public opinion in their favour...They want a stable society which allows them to maintain their positions.[36]

It is these characteristics and the basic need for social stability that makes them the political rear guard. Thus, while the existence of a middle class is apparent, China still does not have a middle class or a civil society as an 'agent of change'. Instead, they have closely associated themselves with the goals of the party in the name of stability and to maintain the status quo.

---

33. Qiu Liping, "A study and Discussion of Social Strata in Chinese Cities Today – Taking Shanghai as an Example", *Social Sciences in China*, Spring 2002, p. 79.
34. Qiu Liping, "A study and Discussion of Social Strata in Chinese Cities Today – Taking Shanghai as an Example", *Social Sciences in China*, Spring 2002, p. 79.
35. Zhou Xiaohong, "Zhongchan Jieji: Heyi keneng yu Heyi ke wei?" (The Middle Class, Is It Possible and Is It Necessary?), *Sociological Seminar,* Dept. of Sociology, Nanjing University, no. 15, Sept. 18, 2002, p. 18.
36. Zhou Xiaohong, "Zhongchan Jieji: Heyi keneng yu Heyi ke wei?" (The Middle Class, Is It Possible and Is It Necessary?), *Sociological Seminar,* Dept. of Sociology, Nanjing University, no. 15, Sept. 18, 2002, p. 16.

Basic Problems of Social Stratification and the State's Policy Responses

Let me now turn to my final question. That of the State's responses to this emerging socially stratified society. China has undoubtedly made impressive economic gains over the last two decades and according to recent statistics managed to pull 220 million people out of poverty.[37] However, the miracle is marred by the increasing gap between rich and poor, both regional and within regions. Fan Gang, for example, points out "how China has now entered a new and more painful stage of development where the contradictions are clearly visible. In a recent article published in the official People's Daily:

> The development process of many countries shows that during this stage two development results may appear. In one scenario, a country successfully industrialises and modernises. In another, growing economic gaps and social tensions "cause development to stagnate, or even result in turmoil and regression."[38]

Today China's leadership is painfully aware of the increasing social disparities in China and knows that if not tackled immediately, can lead to large scale social instability in the near future. Already, reports of protests by laid off workers, the spiraling incident of crime and even reports of people dying of hunger are common and were put at more than 90,000 last year. Apart from this the poor record on work safety, the dying of miners, forcible land dispossession in the name of development followed by inadequate compensation, is beginning to hurt the image of the party.

The government has responded by making a policy change in its earlier concentration of focussing singularly on GDP growth. Today it is trying to initiate debate and discussion about slowing down economic growth so that funds can be freed for social welfare programmes and redirected at building a collapsing rural health and education sector. It is also encouraging the emergence of NGO's and other civil groups that can locally tackle the problems faced by the poorer sections of society. When I was in China last November, for example, the local press was full of how an NGO had gone to court on behalf of migrant labourers in

37. Kuhn, Anthony, "The death of growth at any cost", *Far Eastern Economic Review*, April 2004, p. 28.
38. *People's Daily*, 21 Feb 2004.

the construction industry who had not been paid wages for a year. The NGO won the case, a first of its kind. This of course, would not have happened had the Party not supported the initiative. In fact, migrant labour is really the main problem in cities today and the State is making attempts to create more favourable conditions for them. This includes doing away with the household registration system, the main form of control. The state is also trying to put in place an objective legal system to address industrial and other disputes.

Further, it has also attempted to change the role of its frontal organisations such as the All China Women's Federation, the Trade Unions and even the Youth Organisation and has turned them more into organisations that address the needs of newly emerging poor and laid off workers by retraining them and by becoming employment agencies. The government's attempt to develop the Western region through infrastructure development and other forms of resource allocation is also one of the ways it is seeking to balance the growing regional imbalance. At the ideological level, the Xi Jinping team has tried to instill with greater vigour, the idea of eliminating poverty and creating a middle class society by 2050. Associating with the dream of a great and strong China is seen as compensation for the people of China to remain patient and committed to the goals of the party.

A Social Security Policy

A recent and comprehensive book by Kinglun Ngok and Cha Kwan Chan, China's Social Policy Transformations and Challenges[39] offers us interesting new data and information about the State's responses to poverty and social inequalities. They provide us with an overview of how the system of social security works in China.

They see this sector as having three dimensions: first, the state with its related governmental levels. This they describe as fragmented authoritarianism because multiple agencies are involved. Second, there is the local level, where the central-local interaction is vital. Third, and entirely new, is the partial opening given by the state to societal organisations such as NGOs, and even lawyers and scholars.

39. Kinglun Ngok and Cha Kwan Chan (eds), *China's Social Policy Transformations and Challenges*, 2016.

Regarding implementation of social policy, Leung and Xiao's article in the book points out how the first urban based social assistance programme, instituted in response to massive state owned enterprise (SOE) layoffs, was set up in Shanghai in 1992 and called the Minimum Living Standard Guarantee System for urban residents or the *dibao* system. Initially, the recipients numbered 1.8 million in 1998, growing to 21 million in 2013. The average monthly assistance increased from 65 yuan in 2004 to 243 yuan in 2013. In rural areas the national *dibao* system has been in place since 2007. Those qualifying for assistance are locally determined, with local civil cadres relying on residents committees. Wide discrepancies are reported; it is at the verification levels that problems are compounded and corruption seeps in. The authors show that apart from the cash based dibao system, other social schemes such as medical assistance also exist, supporting about 100 million; 60 percent of the support comes from central funds, going up to 90 percent in poorer regions.

In 2013, for example, 39 million applications were granted with an expenditure of 9 billion yuan. Other articles in the book cover old age pensions, labour, health, housing and education support. The pension system is a contributory one, and Peng details three categories: the urban employee basic pensions; new rural social pensions; and the urban resident social pensions. In the basic rural and urban pensions there is a mandatory social pool and an individual element. Amongst employees, there are enterprise annuity schemes and occupational annuity schemes. By 2012, this system was made mandatory. Although figures show a massive increase in enrolment, with 483.7 million rural residents covered in 2012, it suffers from huge inequities due to low levels of individual contributions and lack of personal resources.

Ngok and Xie's chapter shows changes in labour policy with the system of lifelong employment largely replaced by contractual employment. The major change is that labour relations come under the rule of law rather than ideology. The first labour law was enacted in 1994 and, 'represented the state's attempt to create a united labour regime across different types of ownership or firms in the context of market transition' (p. 69). Migrant labour is another key issue. Penalised by the hukou system that limits social services to documented urban residents, migrants lack access to basic affordable housing, education and health facilities. This discrimination also features in an article on education policy. Lin's chapter on rural-urban migration gives insight into the guanxi and patriarchal networks that affect migration. She points out that male out-migration is becoming part of a culture of patriarchal responsibility and a generational tradition.

The chapters on the housing, health and education sectors also stress the emerging inequalities that now exist, since each sector is controlled by the market, although the state now provides low rent and public rental housing. Similarly, rising health costs have in recent decades turned illness into a poverty trap for many in China. We learn that even in the 2000s, 95 percent of the rural population had no health protection. As Wong notes, the centre has been pushing for insurance schemes both collective and individual, but the rate of implementation remains uneven and further privatisation of the sector under Xi Jinping is a worrying trend. The chapter on rural social policy giving us a historic sweep of the changes that have occurred in the manner the state interacts with its rural citizens. The goal in recent decades has been poverty alleviation with the initial focus on the Three Western regions, starting in the 1990s. Despite considerable success, Shi-Jiunn Shi feels that the programmes lack a comprehensive strategy. He sees the conflict as one between the goals of economic growth and social justice. Papers on China's child policy and its disability care tell us that China did not have a policy of child welfare till a judicial framework for child rights was legislated. However, Wan points out that welfare services for children, especially problems of violence and abuse, are limited.

The government owns responsibility only for six categories: orphans, the disabled, prisoner's children, disaster- and aids-affected children, and street children. Other vulnerable categories have not been covered. New NGOs are coming up, and Ma sketches out the policy, control and limits of the NGO sector. The government promotes certain types of NGOs while suppressing others. This also corresponds with the goal of downsizing government social costs by outsourcing certain mid-tier tasks. It also encourages charitable tax-free donations to this sector. He calls it: 'the government purchasing social services from social organisations'. Ultimately, it is Janus-faced politics, and he indicts the government for keeping this sector alive only in service of the state (p. 176).

This informative book provides us with a much needed understanding of the States responses to emerging social tensions and inequalities in the political economy and society of China. Ngok rightly points out that although some gains have occurred, especially in the insurance and rural welfare regime, this policy regime is still highly fragmentary and people's rights to welfare are tightly tied to their household registration system that determines access to social services in urban China and excludes rural migrant labour. Unless a comprehensive reform of the hukou system is carried out, sections of the population like migrant labour and 'left-behind' rural families in poorer regions remain vulnerable to poverty.

Conclusion

In my paper I have argued that China is today a highly stratified society and this is visible on the ground and within intellectual discourse. Unfortunately, data used for this paper is drawn from one of the last comprehensive survey on social inequality that was carried out in China. It remains, despite having being collected a decade ago, extremely valid for the conclusion made. By breaking down the different types of education available and differing access to it, attempts to provide a general overview of the new social reality in China – that of a highly stratified society and the role being played by education in cementing this stratification. This is an area that is going to pose major problems for China and is already fraught with serious ramifications where social stability is concerned because it is creating, especially amongst the poor in urban areas, and amongst the rural areas a large class of underpaid and undereducated people. Whether the Chinese government, through policies, and better resource allocation, can surmount these emerging inequalities remains to be seen. This coupled with lack of social justice mechanisms as provided by a democracy, such as rule of law, trade unions, a free press and civil society action such as that of NGO's as intervening agencies, means that those at the bottom of the pile our left to agitate against the state and often punished and victimized. China has allowed NGO's to intervene in social development but these are controlled by the State very strictly and not encouraged to allow anti-state or state policy questions. To what extent China can balance the needs of specialised, highly educated manpower and its social policies of universal, quality education, is the challenge this sector.

This paper has been based largely on Chinese sources on the subject. Unfortunately, after 2005, no other comprehensive and large scale survey based work is available. China no longer represents the egalitarian and strictly structured social system that it did. Even if one were to look only at the different groups being identified by the Chinese sociologists, a deeper understanding of the social relations evolving within these groups becomes of great significance. Research carried out on the changes experienced by East European socialist societies have also shed light on the type of social changes that result. The work of Kornai is exemplary here.[40] Kornai, stressed the way people's daily interactions changed due to the prevalence of what he calls, 'vertical dependency', where rather than dependence on the self, one relied on the state and its representatives to meet ones material needs. Today, in China this vertical dependency has certainly changed to one where one has to depend on oneself. Chinese society has evolved into a hybrid where vertical control continues to be exercised by the state party apparatus, while survival and security becomes increasingly dependent on horizontal networking. In conclusion, China presents an excellent example of the complexity of social differentiation that occurs when a society undergoes economic and structural change.

Bibliography

Bian, Yanjie, (1994), *Work and Inequality in Urban China,* Albany State University of New York Press, 1994.

-----1994b), "Guanxi and the allocation of Urban Jobs in China", in *China Quarterly,* no. 140: 971-98.

----1997), "Bringing Strong Ties Back In: Indirect Ties, Network Bridges and Job Searches in China". *American Sociological Review,* 62, 366-85.

Bourdieu, P (1987), *An Outline of a Theory of Practice,* Cambridge University.

Huang Ping (1993), "Intellectuals seeking a destination while drifting aimlessly" *Zhonguo Shehui Kexue,* 1993, no. 2.

Kornai, Janos (1992), *The Socialist System: The Political Economy of Economism,*

40. Janos Kornai, *Highways and Byways, Studies on Reform and Post-Communist Transition*, (Cambridge: MIT Press, 1995).

Princeton University Press, 1992.

-(1995) *Highways and Byways, Studies on Reform and Post-Communist Transition,* MIT Press, Cambridge, 1995.

Kinglun Ngok and Cha Kwan Chan (eds), *China's Social Policy Transformations and Challenges,* Routledge, 2016.

Kuhn, Anthony, (2004), "The death of growth at any cost". In *Far Eastern Economic Review,* April, pp. 28-31.

Li Lulu (1999) "On Social Stratification", *Shehuixue Yanjiu,* No. 3.

Li Peilin (1995), "Structure of Classes and Strata and the Changes in Interest Structure in the New Era", *Zhongguo Shehui kexue,* No. 3.

Li Peilin (1995), *Report on Classes and strata in the new era in China,* Liaoning Peoples Publishing House.

Li Peilin (2002), "Introduction: Changes in Social Stratification since the Reform", *Social Sciences in China,* Spring, pp. 43-47.

Li Chunling (2002), The Class Structure of China's Urban Society during Transition" in *Social Sciences in China,* spring, pp. 91-99.

Li Chunling & Chen Guangjin (2002), "Report on the Social Stratum and Structural Changes," in *Blue Book of Chinese Society*, Social Science Publishing House, Beijing, pp. 115-132.

Li Qiang (2002), "New Changes in Social Stratification" in *Blue Book of Chinese Society,* Social Sciences Document Publishing House, Beijing. pp. 133-143.

-------(2001), "Conflicting Occupational Prestige Evaluations in the Transitional Period in China", *Social Sciences in China,* spring.

Liu Xin (2002), "Strata Consciousness in Transformation-era Urban China," in *Social Sciences in China,* spring, pp. 81-89.

Jiang Liu (ed) (2002), *Blue Book of Chinese Society,* 2002. Social Sciences Documentation Publishing House, Beijing.

Riskin, C (1987), *China's political economy: The quest for development since 1949,* Oxford, Oxford University Press.

Ruan, Danqin et.al (1997), "On the changing Structure of Social Networks in Urban China" *Social Networks,* 19, 75-90.

Solinger, D.J, "Urban Entrepreneurs and the State: The Merger of State and Society", (1992) Arthur Rosenbaum (ed.) *State and Society in China: The Consequences of Reform,* Boulder Press.

Qiu Liping (2002), A study and Discussion of Social Strata in Chinese Cities Today –Taking Shanghai as an Example", in *Social Sciences in China,* spring, pp. 69-80.

Stockman, N (2000), *Understanding Chinese Society,* Oxford, Polity Press.

Sun Liping (1996), "Relations, Social Relations and Social Structure". *Shehuixue yanjiu,* 1996, no. 5.

--------- (2002), "Reaccumulation of Resources: The Back-ground of Social Stratification in China in the 1990s" *Social Sciences in China Today,* spring.

Thakur, Ravni (2002), "The reform of the Hukou Zhidu: A Comment," *China Report,* Vol. 38, issue 2, pp. 299-306.

Yang Yiyong and Xinxiaobai (2002), "Status and Trends in Income Distribution" in *Blue Book of Chinese Society, 2002,* Social Sciences Document Publishing House, Beijing. pp. 144-164.

Yun Kangpan (1989), *Shehui xuezhi dui Shehui de jinggao* (Warnings about society from sociologists) Beijing Chinese women's publishing house.

Yu Heping (ed.) (2002), *Zhongguo gongmin shehui de xingqi yu zhili de bianyan,* CASS, Beijing.

Zhang Wanli (2002), "Twenty years of Research on Stratified Social Structure in Contemporary China", *Social Sciences in China,* spring *Zhongguo shehui kexue yuan* (1994).

The project Group of Chinese Private Entrepreneurs, "Operation of the Chinese Private Enterprises and the Group Characteristics of Private Enterpreneurs", in *Zhongguo Shehui kexue,* No. 4, pp. 60-76.

Zhou Xiaohong (2002), "Zhongchan Jieji: Heyi keneng yu Heyi ke wei? (The Middleclass, is it possible and is it necessary?" *Sociological Seminar No. 15,* Sept 18, Dept. of Sociology, Nanjing University.

Note: The large data base used in this article is from a decade ago since this was the last large scale social science survey carried out by Chinese researchers and openly available. The trends identified continue to cause issues.

Chapter - V

Rethinking Development: A Review Article on Tibet and Xinjiang

Introduction

Any discussion concerning itself with the development or the politics of Tibet since China started its ambitious Western Development Strategy (*Xibukaifa*), immediately enters into a debate between two separate narratives that run counter to each other. For the Chinese policy-maker and for Chinese middle class opinion, Tibet is seen as a pampered part of China, one that gets amongst the highest percentage of state subsidy and yet agitates for separation under the influence of the 'splittist' and 'anti-nationalist', Dalai Lama. They also cite the impressive gains made in the standards of living in this region due to the large investments in infrastructure made by the State. Any regional inequality is blamed on cultural factors and on the inability of the Tibetans to benefit from economic modernisation due to a lack of work culture and their traditional mind sets. The Chinese state argues that its large minority provinces of Xinjiang and Tibet have had problems because of lack of development and offers economic development as the panacea to solve any dissatisfaction prevalent amongst the populations of this region. This position has been supported by research carried out by Chinese academics and also international researchers (1).

The other side of the narrative questions not just the history of Tibet being a part of China, but also the supposed gains made by Tibetan's through the development policies that have been put in place by the government of China. They point out that the Chinese government policies have led to nothing but the marginalisation of the Tibetan population, the rapid influx of Han migrants to the Tibetan plateau, and a persistent attempt to annihilate Tibet's indigenous culture. According to this view, the integration of Tibet into the mainstream of Chinese economy should be viewed as a colonial process. This position receives support from the Tibetan diaspora and now, from academic research, carried out in Tibet over the last decade.

Two books published recently have shed more light on the politics of development in Tibet. These are Stephen Fischer's, *The Disempowerment of Development* and Emily T. Yeh's *Taming Tibet.* Both books are based on extensive field work and both scholars have spent long years working in their own respective fields, developmental economics for Fischer and geography and spatial ethnographic studies byYeh. Both books explore the complicated narratives that seek to define the Tibet question within the wider critique of Development theories as a whole. While coming from separate disciplines, ethnography and development studies, both scholars help us better understand the processes of marginalisation of the community taking place in Tibet today, and more importantly, both books emphasize the same result of development politics and policy in contemporary Tibet. They argue that increasing political and economic marginalisation is today the direct result of Chinese policy based as it is on development narratives that promise a better life and standards of living, while ignoring the dynamics that may exacerbate disempowerment of ethnic groups.

The Processes of Marginalisation in Tibet

The major contribution of both books to the ongoing debate of marginalisation of the Tibetan community is the broad theoretical sweep of development theory that the books take. Fischer arrives at his conclusions by examining the political economy of Tibet through a 'development vs empowerment' paradigm. While accepting that development has certainly taken place in Tibet and has led to declining poverty levels and a betterment of overall human development indicators, he concentrates on the political and economic strategies that the Chinese state has used to integrate and assimilate Tibet within the macro Chinese economic growth strategy. His field work is done through the nineties and continues into the twenty first century, a period when economic modernisation and rising standards of living became the goal and the tradeoff the Chinese Communist Party made with its citizens, security and wealth vs freedom or democracy. Divided into nine chapters, the first two chapters of the book are devoted to a historical sweep of Chinese development strategies for this region. He shows how right from the mid-fifties, Tibet becomes an important strategic zone for China, thus influencing the approaches taken by planners for this region. He points out, in chapter two, how the integration of Tibet was not without a great deal of resistance and blood shed, starting with the resistance to the hiving off of Qinghai and its merger into Gansu under the active collaboration of the Nationalist government and Muslim warlords such as Ma Bufang in the 1930's. After Communist annexation, resistance was led by the Kham's of Amdo till the uprising in 1959 and the escape of the Dalai Lama to India.

The 60's are characterised by the politics of Mao and the overall attack on religion that peaked during the Cultural Revolution, with many monasteries and religious relics destroyed. Ethnic identities were seen as subversive and as detracting from the great communist comradeship and loyalty to Mao. This strategic dimension and Tibet's consistent retrieval and emphasis on a separate Tibetan identity have determined the larger political discourse on Tibet within China.

The book takes special note of the nature of Han labour migration into Tibet by examining how marginalisation gets institutionalised in Tibet through rapid labour transitions leading to the perennial fault lines that continue between urbanisation and Hanisation on the one hand and a largely, 90 percent, rural Tibetan population. Here he echoes Yeh's conclusions that spatiality plays a very large role in the marginalisation of the Tibetan population when he says, "Urbanisation sets the stage for understanding the crux of modern ethnic tensions". However, he takes issue with the generally accepted idea of large scale migration of Han's to the region. He points out that most of this is transitional and fewer Han chose to become permanent settlers in Tibet, unlike in Xinjiang (104). This is an important insight and corroborated by any visit to Tibet where one notices how the Han dominate all urban sectors and how the spatial distance is also an economic distance.

Fischer then examines the close linkages between employment and education today that is further disenfranchising the Tibetans under this State led strategy of modernisation. Economic opportunities are directly linked to the knowledge of Chinese even for those willing to invest in any tourism or other adventure. Thus, while economic growth and development is certainly taking place, they are not necessarily empowering or enriching the Tibetan population.

Forced sinisation, is thus the main strategy being employed by the Chinese state to bring about further unity or the 'assimilationist agenda' of the Chinese as Fischer calls it (251). This schooling and skills imbalance is ensuring that Tibetans lose out on the new jobs being created in a new economy and forces them into the unskilled low paid manual labour sector due to their having only basic primary education and that too in Tibetan. Fischer has marshaled an enormous data base to substantiate his argument and leaves little doubt about the long term and growing asymmetry in education and employment that will arise if this trend continues. Showing a survey by gender from 2009, he shows how 47.2% of women and 24.3% of men are still illiterate in the 13 and older age group of Tibetans. The statistics for China are 1.1.% for men and 4.1% for women (259). This is a keystone of his argument about disempowerment through development and a very valid perspective because it puts Chinese discourse on development into perspective.

Tibetan's rejecting these attempts to embrace Chinese language and culture, can thus, actually been seen as a form of resistance as the book documents when it looks at sites of resistance and examines the religious networks emanating out of Tibetan Buddhism as counter strategies of integration. It concludes by exploring how processes of polarisation can lead to strategies of resistance, as is the case in contemporary Tibet. Religion and resistance become closely interlinked and provide alternative networks of livelihood, cultural regeneration and passive opposition to the Chinese project of integration. A rejection of integration is not turning away from development per se but merely an expression of agency even if it means continued marginalisation.

Yeh's book corroborates the work of Fischer as she too speaks of this 'strategy of integration' by delving into the politics of land transformation in Tibet and how spatial planning has been one of the means through which the identity of traditional cities and populations has been transformed. Her field work too is carried out during the late

20th and early 21st century. Yeh's ethnographic study and very visual narrative is important here as she explores the dynamics of spatial power in the new housing and infrastructure projects, from highways to rail routes that have strengthened Tibet's integration with China like never before. Divided into three long sections, further subdivided into chapters, Yeh's work covers both geography and anthropology as she includes personal impressions and lengthy interviews with her subjects. These are an excellent complement to the more statistical study of Fischer. Yeh uses a wide swathe of theoretical literature, both sociological and development to link patronisizing strategies of development as a civilisational favour. She calls it, using Marcel Mauss's category of the power of gift, to show how the Chinese majority sees development as a 'gift' to the backward Tibetans. Theoretically she places the 'gift' as a strategy of discursive power meant to ingratiate the recipient, in this case, the Chinese state with its gift of development for backward Tibet. In her study we are able to see the effect of state power and how it shapes and influences the daily lives of the indigenous population.

Yeh starts by examining the politics of land and the early period of land appropriation by the Chinese state. This chapter is extremely interesting, based on interviews with workers who participated in commune labour during the fifties and sixties and shows how land reorganisation plays a major role in strengthening state control in Tibet. Her largely ethnographic study divides Chinese strategies of development into chapters that deal with land, plastic and then the stage of concrete in the transformation of the Tibetan landscape and its spatial hierarchies. She then goes on to examine how the vectors of development change after China's 21st strategy of Western Development that has seen migration as a major component of transfer of development. Migrants are seen as a positive force by the state and as agents of technological transfer. They are also seen as essential for pushing modernisation in the otherwise backward region, a position that Yeh counters through her field work, showing how migrant labour instead of passing on new skills, has little contact with the Tibetan population. Here she examines the role played by vegetable farmers from Sichuan who have been at the forefront of commercial agriculture in Tibet, leading her to title her chapter, "The Making of

Little Sichuan". She points out how Han farmers come in, rent land, make their seasonal money and leave. They have little to do with the local population, let alone transfer any skills. They sell to and deal with other Han migrants.

Finally, she talks of the current politics of land and the discourse of development that sees urbanisation and concrete housing as necessary to effect long lasting changes in the socio-politics of the region. She examines in detail the transformation of rural land into urban industrial and housing projects and how this has transformed life-styles of the indigenous population, albeit not always positively. She also brings out how this discourse of development in Tibet is spatially structured to create separateness between the Han and the Chinese, and how all development is seen as a gift by the state that should be reciprocated by unquestioning loyalty by the Tibetans. Thus, both books corroborate each other albeit emphasizing different aspects of China's overall strategy of assimilation. They both point out that the local Tibetan population is at an increasing disadvantage, the different elements of which we shall discuss in detail.

Integration, Urbanisation and Marginalisation

China started its Western Development Strategy since the ninth five year plan in 1996, a policy designed to take the benefits of its impressive and overall economic growth in coastal regions to the Western part of its boundaries, the provinces of Xinjiang and Tibet. This policy has two parts, one large infrastructure development in the region to increase connectivity with the rest of China, and two, encouraging its coastal states and companies to come and invest in this region. This Western region also happens to be peopled by minorities and is a contested space, that has seen enormous dissent and rioting in both Xinjiang and Tibet, already testifying to issues of identity as a major cleavage in the region.

Any visit to Tibet and Xinjiang shows how infrastructure development and large scale industrial and tourism projects have sprouted. Signs of 'development' are visible in the roads, the hotels, new apartment blocks springing up against the deep brown green oasis that makes up Lhasa. There are shops and malls and internet cafes. Encouraging and incentivising coastal China to invest in the provinces of Xinjiang and Tibet. It is this infrastructure development that Yeh sees as the spatial dimensions of State power and its capacity to reorganise land use and community displacement. She further points out how these projects, linked directly to urbanisation, have transformed Lhasa and created two cities, the emerging concrete housing blocks and apartment complexes, increasingly inhabited by migrating Han and Hui (Muslim Chinese), while Tibetan villages move further into the interiors. It is however, also creating a privileged Tibetan class, made of government employees who are being housed in modern rebuilt villages, often built by Chinese land developers and subsidized by the State.

Fischer, too, has systematically demonstrated that this overall development strategy has not necessarily 'empowered' the Tibetan population. He goes further and questions the whole paradigm that creates for, Chinese minorities, a discourse of subsidies, and integration based on vertical dependence, replicating the power relations inscribed in the center periphery models of development and economic integration the world over. Fischer questions this model and its articulation in Tibet to show how this development strategy may result in a general improvement in the lives of people, and accepts that this has certainly been the case in Tibet, but ultimately it is a strategy that leads to disempowerment and limits the options of the local population for upward social mobility and access to resources, decision-making and identity. It also results in, what he calls the dynamic of 'boomerang aid', that is subsidies largely return to the center while debilitating indigenous forms of wealth creation and accumulation in most sectors, apart from the rural and subsistence economy (p. 30). He argues that the coexistence of marginalisation and rapid economic growth in Tibet are not exclusive. Instead, he shows how they represent processes occurring through all social hierarchies and are built into the very dynamic of growth. He argues that politics apart, the case for disempowerment in Tibet needs to be studied and debated from this theoretical perspective. He points out that assimilation, both economic and linguistic can, instead, lead to greater structural discrimination rooted in fundamentally unequal power relations.

Fischer marshals an enormous amount of data, both field visits to Tibet and areas with Tibetan populations such as Qinghai, and details the different aspects of budgetary allocations to show that the aid and subsidy driven development of Tibet has certainly improved the material lives of the people and also their health and education levels, nevertheless, the loss of identity and grievance felt by the people of Tibet have continued to accumulate, turning them into passive objects of development with little or no participation.

In essence, Fischer argues that the intensified economic integration of Tibet into the regional and national development strategies on 'assimilationist' terms, has in turn intensified various dynamics of subordination and marginalisation faced by the Tibetans of all social strata and despite the evident material improvements in their living standard', (p.9). Conceptually, Fischer locates his thesis of marginalisation in Tibet as based on the same patterns of growth and development shown in the center – periphery relations of power, acknowledging his debt to scholars such as Preibisch, Furtado and Sunkel. In this respect, marginalisation and subordination are not necessarily associated with absolute or even relative indicators of poverty and material deprivation. Instead, they occur at the level of status, spatial and linguistic difference, raising wider sociological issues of ethnicity and power, further resonating in the identity politics of resistance.

Yeh reaches similar conclusions in her research as she documents the transformation of land use and the disintegration of the old political economy based around the monastic system. Grounding herself on the Foucaldian notions of spatial arrangements as part of the discursive power of the state to control its population, she states, "In development regimes, ruling powers claim progress as goal, a certain peoples or population as the object of improvement and offer an ideology to both achieve and measure progress."(p.13). It is this notion of governing bodies through the effects of power, she takes from Foucault to argue that state power is not merely oppressive but is subject forming and includes consent. This reification of state power is linked to Foucault's notion of disciplinary regimes. She uses her work to show how "state power has been produced through the control over social space since the 1950's through the material transformation of the landscape" (p.32). She points out that these disciplinary practices are common across the state of China and in other states but "are employed to an extraordinary degree in Tibet…In Lhasa, these practices include not only rules of spatial partitioning segmentation and registration, and controls on mobility but also the heightened visibility of the State's capacity for violence, displayed through the more than dozen military and paramilitary garrisons sitting within the urbanised core of the city" (p.34). She, clearly spells out the discrimination faced by the indigenous Tibetans due to these spatial hierarchies.

Yeh examines the practices of state surveillance through the organisation of space and residence, as also the results that lead to internal surveillance of the self by the Tibetan populations, who have learnt to define safe and unsafe places. It is the private family space that becomes a site of counter narratives of Tibetan history and politics. Circumambulations around temples, and other sacred spaces also continue to provide alternative narratives to the state controlled discourse of development and scientific progress. Thus for Yeh, space is both an exercise of power and a site of resistance. Here again, both Fischer and Yeh complement each other's research, showing how once again, religion becomes the face of resistance.

Creating New Social Hierarchies

Both books converge in their documentation of the difference, spatial and economic, that exists amongst the Tibetan population and the increasingly visible and more prosperous urban Han population, leading to effective marginalisation of the indigenous population. Yeh looks at the migration of peasants from Sichuan who come into Tibet, lease plots of land as vegetable farmers and pay rent for the season, often returning to Sichuan during the winter months. She terms this the 'plastic phase of development' as hothouses under plastic sheets sprung up around Lhasa. She, however clearly spells out the discrimination faced by the indigenous Tibetans due to these spatial hierarchies. She also points out that this is not forced migration but choices made by peasants from neighbouring provinces as labour mobility becomes a key component of market reform. Land is leased by Tibetans owners for cultivation and they derive rent from this activity. However, Yeh points out how this activity is also leading to a discourse of the 'lazy Tibetan', unable and unwilling to cultivate their own land. She found Tibetans echoing this discourse in a self-deprecatory manner, thereby accepting the discourse of the dominant community and more importantly, the reasons they hire migrant Han labour if they have any business of farming concerns.

She starts her discussion with the original land reform movement in the fifties when the Chinese PLA ran commune farms to ensure regular food supply to its troops stationed there and shows how the initial movement actually transformed positively, the poorer Tibetan's relationship to land. Through oral histories of old Tibetan commune workers, such as on the July First State Farm, she knows how they actually felt they had bettered their lives since most of them were servants to monasteries and serfs. Thus, in her assessment, the early part of Chinese takeover may have been contested by the elite, but was certainly welcomed by the serf class that found itself suddenly necessary and elevated to honour. The earlier Chinese migrants and PLA too were different, idealistic in their own revolutionary discourse, representing a class equality and not a ethnic inequality. Like, Fischer, she however, finds, that today's market socialism has had no empowering effect on the Tibetans, instead leading to greater marginalisation as they are unable to compete at the educational or skill levels with the demands of the new economy.

Speaking specifically of the linkages between employment and education, Fischer echoes the key role played by the linkage of Chinese language, educational qualifications and the current job market, whether in the state or within the private sector. In his research, like Yeh he finds, that Han Chinese generally tend to discriminate on 'cultural or linguistic grounds or on the grounds of patriotism'. As he argues, 'marginalisation is better understood as being continuously reproduced within development through the manner by which peripheral and disadvantaged populations are integrated into broader national or even global processes.'

Yeh too speaks of the forms of discrimination that seep into the cultural discourse of Tibet, where even the Han who have lived too long in Tibet are looked down upon in their own native places. Thus, more and more, we find within development discourse, the necessity to speak of more sociological concepts such as hierarchies of power and status. Or the composite that makes up what, Bourdieu calls, symbolic power. This spatial and economic stratification, that both scholars document, is easily visible in the urban regions of Lhasa, even on a casual visit. The shop owners, the taxi drivers and the large number of tourists are Han Chinese. The Tibetans are often the waitress's, the rickshaw pullers and the shop girls. As a Chinese hotel owner told me, "*Tsampa he mi hede bulai'*, Rice (the Chinese staple) and Tsampa (the Tibetan staple) don't mix well!

Fischer and Yeh, in different ways, link this center periphery development strategy to the inception of modernisation in Tibet once the Communist Party established its direct control over Tibet in the 1950s, and explores the role played by ideology and religion in the construction of modern Tibetan nationalism. Fischer points out that historically, especially from the 13th to the 19th centuries, three ethnic groups interact in this region, the Tibetans who owned all the land wealth and power in Tibet, the Muslims from western China, who were largely merchants and traders and the Han who had very little if no presence in the region before 1950. He notes that an important shift takes place in Han –Tibet relations after the collapse of the Manchu dynasty that had until then dealt with Tibet. For the first time, the Han, responding to the overall rise of Han nationalism in the early twentieth century, take control of overall policy towards their neighbours and seriously start to challenge local authority and more importantly, become the representatives for all China in the international arena thus eroding traditional ethnic coexistence, leading to the current ethnic tensions in the region.

China's strategies of minority integration are tied closely to the ideological blueprint laid out by Stalin in the Soviet Union, where minorities were characterised as largely to be brought into the mainstream through development and integration and as Yeh points out, in China, through the idea of 'raising the quality or *suzhi* of the population'. Within this framework, Tibet was analyzed as a feudal society with its population immersed in serfdom and the economy largely subsistence based. Ethnic and religious identities were, thus, reflections of a backward, pre-modern economic base and would eventually recede as economic development accelerated. Unfortunately, under the programme of radical Maoism through the sixties, ethnic identities would come under severe strain as monasteries were destroyed and landholding groups were eliminated. This destruction also destroyed the traditional financial and economic structures of the region, linked as they were to the Monastic system. Instead, the Maoist strategy of pushing industrialisation into the hinterland, known as the Third Front Strategy, was implemented. Tibet also acquired a far greater strategic significance after the 1962 war with India and led to massive development of military related industrial units and infrastructure. Since economic development under Mao was linked to the ideological destruction of religion and religious practices, religious freedom became associated with political freedom and this has remained the case till today, with monks and nuns at the forefront of struggle against Chinese assimilation strategies. The suppression of religion also turned its practice by Tibetans into a form of active resistance to the attempts at integration engineered by the Chinese state.

Demographic Structural Changes: The Causes of Marginalisation

Fischer also draws attention to specifically demographic structural changes to further highlight his conceptualisation of disempowered development. He identifies three factors of population that have had enormous impact on Tibet. These include demographic transitions, urbanisation and increased non-Tibetan migration from other parts of China, especially Han migration. Fischer deals with this subject judiciously pointing out that this Han in migration is largely restricted to urban areas and even here, the Han are more job based migrants, concentrated in urban and mining centers, leaving when their terms are finished rather than permanent settlers. Yeh too points out how Han migration does show a seasonal trend where agricultural labour is concerned, and the rural population remains largely Tibetan but in cities, migration is taking on a more permanent nature as Chinese investment in urban tourism and leisure starts expanding. Thus, any development strategy that takes an open market economy and urbanisation as its parameters of growth, will inevitably, leave out those who like the Tibetans, do not integrate.

Fischer and Yeh both point out that the spatial and economic difference between the Han and the Tibetan populations has led to a greater feeling of discrimination in urban areas. He points out that the official population of Tibetans in TAR stands at 5.42 million according to the 2000 census. He focuses on urban exclusionary dynamics by showing statistics for rural and urban ethnic populations. He points out that within the TAR region, Tibetans make up 84.8% of the rural population but only 9% of the population of towns and 5.8% of the population of cities. The Han Chinese make up 35% of town populations and 44% of the population of cities in the region. The other ethnic group of interest in the region and one that Fischer identifies as important is the Hui or Chinese Muslims who make up 25.6% of the population of towns and are the majority in cities at 54%. He further contrasts these trends with Han migration to other minority areas such as Mongolia and Xinjiang where migration started earlier and was largely agrarian. Thus, Fischer argues that news of Han population swamping the Tibetans must be taken with a pinch of salt especially since rural areas remain largely Tibetan. It is the increasing rural-urban divide, with its obvious ethnic nature that will continue to impede any genuine project for inclusive development.

Nevertheless, as both Yeh and Fisher point out, this also confines Tibetans to the subsistence economy, although, as he argues, they are often rich in asset ownership such as herds. Population movements of the Han during the reform period have been largely to the prosperous coastal regions, despite massive incentives being given for people to settle permanently in the Western regions. He also points out how military personnel are a significant population of Han in the region. Finally, he shows how the appearance of increasing Han or Muslim presence in Tibet or eastern Tibet outside of TAR is largely in urban areas and there is a more market oriented character to the migration. Thus, the crucial issue for Fischer is not whether the Han are flooding Tibet, but that they are starting to dominate the market based employment opportunities that are emerging in urban areas where most of development is taking place.

This employment based discrimination, and therefore the being excluded from market based global economic integration, is linked to the issue of language and education, pointing out how lack of knowledge of Chinese or adequate competence in the language, keeps Tibetans out of urban employment, both within the state sector (now largely run along market lines) and within the private sector. These exclusionary practices have become more pronounced since 2001 when guaranteed employment for graduates was replaced by a supposedly more competitive and merit based hiring. This has had a marked adverse effect on the chances of Tibetan urban graduates who lost out to better educated Chinese speaking Han and Hui. Again, lack of tertiary training in the industrial and construction sectors too ensures that they miss out on jobs in this other growth sector. He points out how even Tibetan monasteries tend to employ Han companies. Thus, while rural areas remain largely Tibetan dominated and still linked to traditional economic networks, it is the urban areas that are becoming place of conflict and contestations. Urban Tibetans are not just the elite amongst Tibetans, these are groups that have cooperated in accepting the wider contours of assimilation, learning Chinese and entering the fields of education in different streams. Assimilative policies also hit a glass ceiling where position of governance within the Party hierarchy and executive positions within the government of Tibet are concerned. All senior positions are Han held and in fact, management of Tibet counts as a major boost for higher positions within the Central government.

The Discourses of Difference

Spatial and economic discrimination, as Yeh points out, also leads to an assumed difference in the comparative **suzhi** or quality of the population. The Tibetans are seen as lazy, incapable of hard work, incapable of speaking Chinese and above all, since the pre-olympic rioting of 2008, as ingrates and not deserving of any special consideration. Yeh calls this the Cultural politics of Development and effectively shows how Tibetan's are regularly stereotyped in both state and public Han discourse. This is visible as one of the vectors of development in Tibet. Being a geographer, Yeh makes special note of the effects of urbanisation on both Tibetan conceptions of their own identity in response to the idea of civilisation now meaning urban life-styles. In her chapter 6 on "Building a Civilised City: Making Lhasa Urban", Yeh shows how building cities and urbanisation, in any case is seen as the natural trajectory of growth and these developments are privileged through financial and other aid from the state.

In the name of development and of building better housing, traditional quarters and community life is being systematically displaced. She points out that the ousted have no choice in the matter. They are losing their farmlands to urbanisation and along with that, their traditional spatial and community moorings. Although the State has provided subsidies, it has still meant that Tibetans have had to borrow money or sell land leases to rebuild new homes demanded by the state to show progress and higher standards of living. She points out how urbanisation is seen as the only way to develop Tibet and bring it on par with the rest of China. But it is precisely this urbanised space and its market economy that is leading to the discursive and material marginalisation of the population and a loss of their traditional community life built around single story houses, agriculture and cattle. Further, Yeh shows, how the Lhasa Development Plan, while unilaterally acquiring land for development, whether for roads or housing areas, is leaving the compensation for any loss to the China based large scale development companies. Loss of farm land and land based economies means that this urbanised Tibetans will now have to find means of earning an income in an urban economy, something that is proving increasingly difficult as they compete in the open market with better qualified Han immigrants.

In terms of economic activity, Fischer marks out another ethnic divide that seems to be growing in urban areas, especially in Tibetan majority regions outside of the TAR such as Qinghai and Amdo. This is the cultural conflict and stereotyping occurring between the Hui Muslim population of the region and the Tibetans. Based on extensive field work in the region, Fischer points out how cultural and culinary taboos dominate the interaction between these two communities. He speaks of the Hui being seen as polluters. These myths have in the past led to the boycotting of Hui business's in these regions. These negative images are now being further fuelled as the Hui, traditional merchant classes, dominate in the commercial sector as traders, challenging Tibetan entrepreneurs and merchants. In contrast, Fischer speaks of the growing relationship amongst the Han and the religious elite within Tibetan society through the reemergence of Buddhism in China and growing interactions with Tibetan Buddhism. The Chinese government, has over the past decade, encouraged the revival of Buddhism and has started training of monks to run the various monasteries being reopened and even converted into tourist sites. China is also playing a greater role in the revival of Buddhist heritage sites in the world such as in Nepal and Sri Lanka.

Fischer states how several monasteries, especially outside the TAR region, have been benefitting from Han donations and Han pilgrims, both from Taiwan and the mainland. He speaks of several Lama's having a following in China and the increasing networking between the Han Buddhists and Tibetan Buddhist clergy. Han monks are even studying and living in Tibetan monasteries. For the Tibetan elite, he sees this as a strategy that helps recreate new networks of hierarchy based on their traditional religious identity.

Assimilative Strategies and Marginalisation

Fischer's and Yeh's books give a comprehensive picture of the history and politics of Tibet's integration within the Chinese economy and the large scale impact of China's assimilative macro policies on the indigenous people and both complement each other. While Fischer concentrates on the policies of economic development and their results, Yeh's ethnography brings out the human element of the story. Her excellent writing and descriptive analysis bring alive the day-to-day changes that are occurring in Tibet. Both books take issue with the politicisation of the field of Tibet studies, especially since any criticism of Chinese policy is identified by the Chinese and criticized internationally with being supportive of the Dalai Lama led struggle for greater autonomy. They point out that scholars have accepted China's claims of economic growth and rising standards of living uncritically and without examining the issues of immigration and cultural and spatial displacement that are taking place in Tibet.

While both scholars accept that this process of marginalisation of select communities and regions is common to developments in other places, they have also highlighted how Tibet is exhibiting a specific character because of the ethnic and cultural differences that form part of the vectors of development. In Tibet, as Fischer and Yeh document, religion and religious identity is closely linked to resistance and protest. Monasteries and monks have always been in the lead, especially in carrying out the very Buddhist form of resistance that does not harm anyone else but protests through immolating the self. Unfortunately, neither author provides any solutions to how States can ensure better standards of living, health and education to all and yet ensure that people do not become mere cogs in the wheel of macro development strategies. The theoretical framework of both books points to an almost inevitable dynamic of marginalisation that operates between dominant and minority groups. In some ways, Fischer does point to the possibility of an alternative relationship between the Han and the Tibetan's if they return to the older networks of Buddhism where the monk, especially the ascetics of Tibet are revered. Fischer shows how these networks are flourishing in Tibetan regions outside the TAR like Qinghai. He shows how individual Chinese are becoming patrons of monks and Buddhism. The revival of Buddhism in China offers a glimmer of hope and may finally lead to the de-demonisation of the Dalai Lama by the State.

Both Fischer's and Yeh's great contribution is not just the development and employment data presented, but the emphasis they place on cultural and linguistic identity as markers of difference and discrimination, raising several questions for any central government run strategy that seeks to assimilate minorities into the dominant whole. Further, both authors make an important corroborative analysis of the limits of development seen merely as a rise in GDP. They bring out the larger issues of empowerment and equality, of status and opportunity. Although Yeh's book is a year older, I chose to read both together because of their complementarities and similar conclusions. Both books are a must read for anybody interested not just in China's relations with its minorities but also other minorities in other countries where states follow hard assimilative strategies.

Issues of development, land rights and identity politics remain important in most multi-ethnic and multilingual communities. India, South America, South East Asia, countries with large migrant populations, all face similar problems and similar debates. We will continue to ask whether local populations should be left untouched, living their lives in consonance with their past cultural practices without the benefits of modern technology or whether the benefits of development should be brought to them through force and top down state programmes. Should people protesting development be seen only in terms of a linear progressive development discourse and as Luddite or should they have the right to their own strategies of identity and resistance through discourses of passive non participation or should they give up identity and amalgamate into a majoritarian whole?

In Tibet it is obvious that participation brings limited reward and not participating brings marginalisation.

Both authors see development by a majority state as hegemonic, a process that forces the minority to collude in their own marginalisation. They also raise important questions about the role played by migration, and it is obvious from their studies, that open migration to minority regions by better educated Han Chinese does lead to the disempowerment of the local Tibetan population, leaving them as uncompetitive for employment in Han run enterprises. Whether the Chinese state will take seriously the increasing and visible disparities and understand the need to discourage large scale migration, remains to be seen. It also needs to create employment opportunities for Tibetan speakers. Both books raise important questions about religion and its role as a force of cohesion and resistance in the specific example of Tibet. It provides an alternative discourse against the onslaught of state led forced assimilation. It becomes the marker of culture and difference. More importantly, they ask whether specificity of cultural practice deserve an overarching universalistic framework of linear development that has always seen raising overall standards of living as empowering. Finally, both books ask important questions of the theory and practice of development, especially if development strategies are state based, and that state dominated by a majority. Is there a way in which States can combine the betterment of human development indicators and yet leave culture untouched? Alas, where Tibet is concerned, the Chinese State is a juggernaut that will not negotiate.

Notes

Andrew Martin Fischer: *The Disempowered Development of Tibet in ChinaA Study in the Economics of Marginalisation,* Lexington Books, Lanham etc, 2014.

Emily T. Yeh: *Taming Tibet: Landscape Transformation and the Gift of Chinese Development,* Cornell University Press, South Asian edition, 2014.

Rong Ma (2010), *Population and Society in Contemporary Tibet,* Hong University Press.

Chapter - VI

Questioning the Practices of Patriarchy: Women's Studies in China

Introduction

The field of academics in China today is radically different from previous years in both content and discipline. The change is especially noticeable in the field of sociology/anthropology and economics. Sociology was banned in the fifties and anthropology reduced to the study of China's minorities. Similarly economics was reduced to a study of Marxian models dominated by the state. Sociology was re-introduced as a university course in 1981 and Fei Xiaotong, one of Chinese prominent social anthropologists was made the Chairman of the Sociology society in 1981.[1] These changes are especially apparent since the nineties. Law and Business Management are other examples of new and popular subjects. China has essentially cut down its list of 'ideologically correct' disciplines.

Women's studies is another subject that has been recently introduced at the University level. Since the nineties, most good universities offer the subject at the post graduate level. Along with this, has been the enormous academic exchanges taking place between China and the world. China has not just integrated its economy with the world, it has also sent its students to study abroad, and unlike during the Mao period, actively encouraged academic exchange

1. Fei Xiaotonbg has done extensive work on China and especially peasant China. His book *From the Soil: Foundation of Chinese Society* (translation of *Xiangtu* by Gary Hamilton, Zheng Wang, Berkley (1990, Berkley University Press), is considered a classic and points out how the social organisation of Chinese society is based on its peasant society that draws both legitimacy and links from an attachment to land.

with the west. This has led to a sea change in the critical perspective within China. Marxism, while still the ultimate safeguard for correct politics, is now challenged by the availability of other theoretical methodologies and critical paradigms.[2]

Women's studies was introduced in China partly as a result of China's growing engagement with different United Nations forums and the availability of funding from these organisations for women's studies. The Beijing Conference held in 1990 on gender issues, is a definite landmark in terms of the legitimacy given to the women's issues within mainstream political and academic thinking. This was the first time that international specialists of women's studies pointed out the radical critical perspectives a gender framework bought to all research. This is not unique to China, Women's studies in the Third World all received a boost with the International Decade of Women and as a result of the second wave of Feminism as it is popularly known.[3]

Feminism, if we define it as one of the new critical paradigms that have emerged post the 1960's, and was influenced to a very large extent by the women's movement and complemented by the new work that emerged in the West, led by Foucault and Derrida and later complemented by the work done by more mainstream scholars like Bourdieu, is certainly a new paradigm in Chinese academia. It has unfortunately not led to a 'woman's movement' that was closely linked to feminism in democratic countries like the West and India, and in fact is the critical difference, but it has allowed the mainstreaming of the idea within the social sciences and within policy planning.

---

2. China under the Maoist regime laboured under a strictly controlled ideological regime where Mao Zedong thought was used as the only methodology to study all subjects. The Cultural Revolution which designated intellectuals as the 'Ninth Stinking' category was the high point of Mao's disdain and dislike for all things intellectual. Today the situation has changed considerably. For more on intellectual climate today, see, Davies, Gloria (ed) (2001) *Voicing Concerns: Contemporary Chinese Critical Inquiry*, Rowman and Littlefield Publishers, Australia.
3. Other Asian countries, such as Thailand, Malaysia, India amongst others also saw an upsurge of NGO's and women's groups dealing with and promoting gender and feminist issues. In China, this was the first time that the government put its weight behind promoting and encouraging women's studies in China. However, China still does not allow any Non-government organisations to exist independently. All NGO's in China have to be affiliated to some government organisation or another. However, the government is encouraging the growth of this sector, especially where social development issues are concerned.

This chapter looks at the emergence of women's studies as a subject and critically examines a women's study reader brought out by the Yunan Minority University Women's Studies programme. This is further complimented by informal conversations with Chinese academics and members of the Women's studies programme. The chapter attempts to contextualise the significance of the emergence of women's studies in China by first examining how this issue was earlier framed, how it is being framed within China and then taking a critical look at its impact both in other disciplines and on the general discursive shift on gender discourse in China.

Earlier Analysis of Women's Subordination in China

Ameliorating the position of Chinese women in traditional society governed by a patriarchal discourse that took its legitimacy from Confucianism with its emphatic privileging of the male or the discourse of **Zhongnan qingnü** (give importance to men and look down upon women) was one of the major demands of the early reformers in China. Although the issue of reforming women's position in society had begun to be debated as early as the 1850's, it was only under the 1898 Palace Reform charter led by mandarins like Kang Youwei that the call to ban customs such as foot-binding and the demand for female education reached a peak.[4] This period coincided with the demise of the China's last Imperial Dynasty, the Qing. The Imperial house was blamed for China's incapacity to face the West and was seen as an anachronism by the educated elite especially of the coastal regions. By the period of the May Fourth Movement, female participation in Education, employment and civil society organisations was on the rise in all the major urban centers. Female education in turned received a fillip being linked to enhancing women's skills for the growing domestic labour market. This period saw the rapid growth of women in the numerous textile mills and factories that dominated Shanghai and other urban cities.[5]

4. Chow Tse-tung's (1966) seminal work on the May Fourth Movement: Intellectual Revolution in Modern China, Harvard University Press, provides an excellent background to the general climate of social reform in early twentieth century China. Also see Croll, Elizabeth (1978) *Feminism and Socialism in China*, Routledge Kegan and Paul, London etc.
5. The entrance of women into factory labour in the early twentieth century was a major social issue and provided both opportunity for peasant and lower

This period can be highlighted as the first attempt to analyse and understand the causes of female subordination in China. The Women's question (**funü wenti**) as it came to be popularly known became part of the wider discourse that represented the forces of democratisation and modernity sweeping China in this period. As Chow tells us, the rallying cry of the early twentieth century was Democracy, Science and Equal Rights for All. Access to the ideas of enlightenment represented by the work of Darwin, Huxley, Mill and others had percolated amongst the educated classes through translations into Chinese. China's rigid social structure and its Confucian ideology was seen as partly responsible for China's defeat at the hands of western powers. Journals such as New Youth, edited by Chen Tuxiu were representative of this radical and new current of thought amongst Chinese intellectuals and youth.[6]

Apart from the liberal ideas of enlightenment, the Marxist perspective and analysis of women's subordination was closely tied to the establishment of the Communist Party in 1921 under the leadership of Chen Tuxiu. Textually, the Communist Party and other left wing intellectuals turned to the work of Marx, Engles and the early Russian women ideologues such as Clara Zetkin and to a lesser extent Alexendra Kollantai influenced the analysis of the women's question in China.[7] Along with the methodology of historical materialism that analysed China as a semi-feudal society, the analysis of female subordination was also couched within the broader parameters of a base/superstructure debate that underpinned early Marxist theory. This was, of course, accompanied by seeing all representations, including religion and that of the sign, gender as mere ideology, and false ideology at that, the real being represented by class.[8]

---

income groups to improve their social status. It also provided the Communist Party its political base amongst women. See, Honing, Emily, (1986). *Sisters and Strangers: Women in the Shanghai Cotton Mills, 1919-1949,* Stanford University Press.

6. Chow Tse-tung (1966), *Op.cit.*
7. Alexandera Kollantai (1872-1952) , an upper class woman, was one of the first to take oin the issue of women's equal rights in the Soviet Union. She was also a writer and scholar of other social issues. See: Croll, *op.cit.*
8. Delia Davin has provided a very positive account of the measures carried out by the Communists to improve the position of women in the areas under their control and also the legislation such as the Marriage Law of 1950. Davin, Delia (1978) *Women Work, Women and the Party in Revolutionary China*, Oxford University Press.

Put simply, patriarchy was tied to private property and it was argued that only the abolition of this base would destroy the superstructure of both patriarchy and class exploitation. In both cases, the struggle for women's equality was inextricably linked to the struggle of the working classes. This subordination of the gender issue to the wider goals of the revolution is reflective in the kind of organisation that the Party creates to represent women. Here Lenin is worth quoting in detail:

> ....Real freedom for women is possible only through communism. This inseparable connection between the social and human position of the woman, and private property in the means of production must be strongly brought out. We must win over to our side the millions of toiling women... there can be no real mass movement without women...Our ideological conceptions give rise to principles of organisation. No special organisations for women: a woman communist is a member of the party just as a man communist with equal rights and duties. Nevertheless we must not close our eyes to the fact that the party must have bodies whose particular duty it is to arouse the masss of women workers, to bring them into contact with the party and to keep them under its influence...(In a conversation with Clara Zetkin 1921).[9]

This set the ideological relationship of the Party's women's organisations with the Party. We must remember that all Communist parties, be they Chinese or Indian, draw their own organisational structure, along with its commitment to 'democratic centralism', from Lenin. He created the Party organisation as a cadre based party, each member controlled by party discipline and a core leadership group at each level in turn answerable to the politburo. Each of the party's various organisations, its trade unions, its women's associations etc were in turn answerable to party line and discipline. Essentially, in practice, this democratic centralism has meant singularity of decision making, the role played by 'leaders', Mao or Stalin, as the final arbitrators of programmers, structures and in China's case, class struggle.

9. Michelle Barrett (1982), "Feminism and the Definition of Cultural Politics", in R. Brunt and C. Rowan (eds) *Feminism, Culture and Politics,* London: Lawrence and Wishart.

Mao's famous Hunan Report lists four oppressions the fourth being patriarchy. As he said:

> A man in China is usually subject to three systems of authority (political authority, clan authority and religious authority). As for women, in addition to being dominated by these three authorities, they are also dominated by men (the authority of the husband). These four authorities – political, clan, religious and masculine – are the embodiment of the whole feudal – patriarchal system and ideology, and are the four thick ropes binding the Chinese people – particularly the peasants.[10]

As far back as 1923 the Party formed a unit dedicated to 'women's work', *funü gongzuo*. This task was handed over to Xiang Jingyu, the first Politburo member of the Communist Party. She was executed in 1927 after being arrested during the anti-communist white terror of this period. During the thirties, after the Communist movement shifted to the countryside, the work of the women's wing was essentially to motivate women to contribute to the war effort. Kay Ann Johnson points out that the work among women was felt to be necessary because in many cases women exercised an influence to join the Red Army.[11] During the period of struggle, women's work essentially focused on motivating women to join the class struggle being waged in rural China. Although major laws such as the marriage law and the right of women to property were promulgated, in practice, their implementation remained uneven. Women were seen as essential for the growth of the productive forces and asked to participate in the anti-war effort. No effort however was made to change the patriarchal discourse and counter the *zhong nan qingnu* ideology. At Yenan too, the Party policy remained the same. Women were organised into production teams and other committees. Stranahan quotes unverified sources to point out that a total of 130,000 women who were members of one association or another.[12]

---

10. *Mao Zedong Collected works,* 1956, Vol. 1, 44 Peoples Publishing House.
11. Kay Ann Johnson, 1983, Women : *The Family and Peasant Revolution in China*. Chicago, University of Chicago. Pp. 52.
12. Patricia Stranhan, "Yenan Women Under the Communist Party. China Researh Monograph no. 27, University of California, Center for Chinese Studies. pp. 45-46.1976: 35 99 Ding Ling is one of the most renowned women writers of the May Fourth Movement and later. She was also an avant-garde feminist who shot to fame in Shanghai for writing controversial stories depicting the

The Party's relationship with the issue of gender equality, can be best summed up by Ding Ling, the well known writer who also worked as editor of the Party's propaganda magazine in Yenan. Ding Ling summed up the double standards of the Party in an article she wrote for the **Jiefang Ribao** on the 8th of March in 1942. According to Ding Ling, women were expected to take on new roles workers and party activists and yet expected to fulfill their responsibilities as wives and mothers. The result was that women were faced with insurmountable problems and derided whatever they did. As she says:

> They were damned for what they did and damned for what they didn't".[13]

If women did not marry they were ridiculed and if they did, they were said to be paying too much attention to their families and self. She went on to say that male leaders should talk less of theory and more of practice. She ended by saying that:

> "if the opinion she was putting forward was that of a male leader they would have been read with great seriousness but unfortunately, being a women, her opinion would probably be dismissed".[14]

Ding Ling was. Mao criticized her personally and she suffered after the hundred flowers movement, spending over twenty years in exile, banned from writing, except on stray scraps. She was subject to criticism within the Party for this and suffered again for her outspokenness during the Hundred Flowers Movement of 1959.

Ideological Limitations

After 1949, once the Communist Party came to power, the Party's woman's organisation was turned into what was defined as a mass organisation. The All China Woman's Federation (ACWF) was formed. The early decades of Communist rule saw several landmark legislative rules passed in favour of equality for women in marriage

---

sexuality of women. She later came to Yennan and helped edit the party paper. See her, *The Diary of Miss Sophie in Collected works of Dingling,* People's Publishng House, 1955, The Latter won the Staling Prize for Literature.

13. *Works of Ding Ling,* People's Publishing House, Beijing, 1982 and The Sun Shines over the Sanggan River, People's Publishing Ding Ling.
14. Ding Ling Speech on the Occasion of Women's Day", 1942, in Croll, E. (1978) *op.cit.*

and in terms of access to education, employment and private property. As Delia Davin points out the Marriage Law of 1950 was one of the most revolutionary laws in China and for the first time created an environment that allowed women the right to leave forced unions of all kinds. Prostitution and, especially child prostitution was wiped out through reeducation campaigns and through the rigid enforcement of health and education norms.[15]

The first decade in the Communist Parties history truly attempted and to a large measure succeeded in undoing centuries of gender subordination. Although the Great Leap Forward and the Cultural Revolution failed as movements, the ideas of gender equality they ushered in were truly revolutionary. The Great Leap Forward with its attempts to communalise housework also attempted to change the impression that woman were responsible for housework and all the traditional attitudes that drew legitimacy from this basic premise. In many ways they did attempt an enforced uniformity where notions of love and sexuality were concerned. However, studies done by both Chinese scholars and International scholars have shown that despite the rhetoric of propaganda and Party/state controlled gender equality remained just as differentiated and unachievable, as it was in countries that employed more democratic structures of social reform and even countries where, like in India, lip service to gender equality was almost obligatory to win elections.[16]

A careful perusal of Chinese Communist history on gender reform also supports this argument. If actual differentials in social participation and salary structures are analysed, one notes that gender discrimination continued at all the same levels that it does in a liberal democracy – i.e. in terms of salary structures, women in leadership positions and even in terms of countering the patriarchal structures inherent within marriage and the idea of the man as breadwinner and woman as housekeeper. One sees clearly that the role of the women's organisations within the party was clearly that of a bridge between women's revolutionary potential as communists and their own gendered exploitation coming second. The chief contradiction

15. Delia Davin, *op.cit.*
16. Mennon, Nivedita (ed), *Gender and Politics in India*, Oxford University Press 1999, Delhi, pp. 374.

was that between classes not between genders. This, we know today, is not an adequate analysis of patriarchy and the culturally justified subordination of women. Men in the Communist Party were not non-sexist or non-patriarchal, forcing a keen debate amongst socialist feminist Marxists internationally. The sixties and seventies was also characterised by several autonomous women's groups that while accepting the importance of women's lack of land and economic rights as fundamental to their rooted subordination, also used the opportunity to point out how patterns of gender subordination at the discursive level and as determinants of social discourse persist despite systemic and economic changes.

This engineered and ideological attempt, backed by state power and its failure to change the fundamental's of gender relations forces us to re-theorise the problem and thereby its analysis. It is here that "Women's Studies" in China is once again bringing out the 'complicated', not easily reducible to paradigms of analysis. Woman as the symbol, the sign, that interlinked discursive grid Foucault talks about, the habitus that Bourdieu does. Gender relations are the primary component of social organisation. This is where women's studies as a discipline comes in as a critical theory, a new paradigm to analyse the different facets of continuing female subordination.

The following section is a critical reading of the subject in China through analyzing the contents and aims of the Women's Studies programme in Yunnan University.

Women's Studies in China Today

1. *Curriculum and Course Content*

The United Nations led Decade for women followed by the Women's Conference in Beijing was an important impetus for the Chinese government to allow for wider critical exchanges about the "Woman Question". Ten years down the line, the syllabus, reach and impact of these women's studies programmes can be assessed. This series of Readers brought out be the Women's studies Programme in the Minority University (*Minzu Daxue*) in Yunnan, is representative of the way the academic discipline is being constructed and the issues that are considered important within China.

The Title of the book is "*Discipline Building of Women's Studies and Minority Women Research*". Published in 2004, the book is a general reader addressed to those pursuing the subject and to the general reader. In this section, I propose to critically read some chosen articles, keeping in mind the comparative context and content of women's studies methodologies and concepts internationally.

The introductory article lays out the "history and development of Women's studies in China Today". Wang Jinling, the author points out how women's studies in China develops during the eighties as part of the universal decade for women, launched by the United Nations".[17] The article is a general historical review and traces the genesis of the Women's question to the May Fourth movement. It becomes more interesting when it delves into the politics behind the establishment of Women Studies programmes. The article points out three main parameters behind the establishment of this discipline at the MA level in China.

1. To put in place a discipline that examines gender discrimination in a long term perspective.
2. Encourage the inclusion of gender sensitive paradigms within the other social science subjects.
3. If included, especially emphasise the methodologies and data collection on all social issues to include the gender perspective. This will enrich the social sciences as a whole.[18]

This is a commendable approach, and in one sense typically mainstream women's studies. Wang Zheng expands the scope of Women's studies to include "A study of different periods of history and examine the way gender relations have transformed and how gender is linked to class....the meaning of women's studies is to promote a new critical theoretical perspective.[19]

At the theoretical level, the main distinction remains that between 'Feminism and Women's Studies'. Here the semantics of the translation

17. Wang Zheng, "Contents and Objectives of Women's Studies" pp. 1-9, p. 5 in Yang Guocai and Ma Shiwen (eds.) *Discipline Building of Women's Studies and Minority Women Research,* (hereafter DBWSMWR)Yunnan Minorities Publishing House, 2004.
18. *Ibid*, p.11.
19. *Ibid*, p. 3.

of concepts such as 'gender studies' (xingbie yanjiu) literally the study of sexual difference, feminist studies (*nuquan zhuyi xue*) literally woman power studies, and then women's studies translated as *Nuxing xue* that is female/women's studies.[20]

This semantic difference is an important clue to the ideological distinction being made between, Feminist studies, seen as essentially American inspired and the more main stream attempts to bring a gender perspective to social science research as a whole. As Wang Zheng says, arguing her case for Gender Studies as the more important definition for this academic discipline:

> Gender Studies (*Shehui xingbie xue*) main thrust is to analyse the social system of gender, the social relations of gender and the relationship between the two genders.[21]

Speaking about the application of the Gender perspective in courses, Zhao and Wang point out that after the 1995 conference, interest in women's studies escalated. This was also the period when writings on feminism started being translated into Chinese. The authors list Wollestoncroft and Beauvoir amongst the classics that were introduced to Chinese readers a this point.[22] The translation of books into Chinese has always been an important indicator of the importance of a subject within the intellectual milieu of China, as was demonstrated in the period prior to the May Fourth Movement of 1919, when the translation of Darwin, Huxley, Marx and others fuelled a social revolution. Women's studies as an academic subject has been revolutionary to the extent that, life the early experience of modernity during the May Fourth, it has widened the terms of the discourse 'woman' and even helped theorise the problems of women within a wider and interlinked discursive network that devolves into the different spaces where the sign 'woman' appears.[23]

The background of teaching staff in women's studies is in different social science disciplines subjects and their chief focus is to carry

20. *Ibid.* p. 5.
21. *Ibid.* p. 5.
22. Zhao Lizhen and Wang Shanshan "The Application of Gender Perspective in Courses, in Yang Guocai and Ma Shiwen", in DBWSMWR *op.cit.* pp. 67-72.
23. On the existential and symbolic experience of modernity in urban cities such as Shanghai, see Wen-hsin Yeh (2000), *Becoming Chinese: Passages to Modernity and Beyond*, University of California Press, 2000.

out gender sensitive research. Staff also interacts with government departments dealing with women's affairs and provides policy inputs. Thus, it also works at the level of a policy think tank. They provide background research and data for projects run by the Women's Departments within different social welfare ministries and also help with the work of the Woman's Federation (*Fu Lianhe*). In general, there was criticism about the work of the Women's Federation amongst the students and staff of the Women's studies center. It was felt that the Federation concentrates only on state sponsored campaign and its outreach to women in general is linked more with government family planning and health programmes rather than in any way questioning or tackling issues of social discrimination.[24]

This emergence of Academic think tanks providing the government with policy inputs is in itself a new phenomenon is China. This has also helped decision making in China transcend the ideological imperatives of the Maoist period to focus on practical strategies of governance and administration. Today, policy think tanks in foreign and social policy have played a large role in redirecting Chinese policy towards pragmatism. China's current emphasis on social development in the countryside is also partly a result of the extensive social science research that has been carried out on the emerging social stratification in China carried out by the social science academy.[25]

Impact on Other Disciplines

The impact of a gender perspective within other main stream disciplines such as sociology as against political science or history, is visible, especially in terms of policy formulation and recommendations. Here a lot of specific projects dealing with women centered research have emerged. The impact of a gender specific perspective is especially apparent in collecting data and statistics on unemployment where we know that more than 60 percent of laid of workers in the past fifteen years have been women above the age of 35.

24. Wang Zheng (2004), *op.cit.*
25. The Academy of Social Sciences published several studies on regional and other emerging inequalities in China and the Chinese government has since then focused attention to rural social development once again. See especially "Social Stratification in China" special issue of *Social Sciences in China Today*, Acadamy of Social Sciences, 2000, October.

Statistics on Education too are gender differentiated like they have always been. However, a look at the sample surveys carried out to study emerging social stratification, did not have gender as a special attribute.[26] Here occupation is often used as the criteria rather than incorporating gender as a subgroup within each survey. This data has to be sifted out of larger surveys on education and employment per se. This is also true for figures to do with poverty and migration. In both areas, region specific figures are not gender specific.[27]

Literature is another area that has seen a huge impact of feminist and gender perspectives. This has in turn fuelled an interesting debate between essentialism and socialisation into gender roles. While critics argue that women's writings has certain special characteristics because they are naturally so inclined, more feminist critics have pointed out how patriarchal such discourse is. Again, literary criticism that moves beyond the boundaries of Marxist socialist realism as the yard stick is new. Here again women centric criticism has pointed out how a gender bias that slots women as writers into stereotypes i.e. women deal mainly with family subjects, women are prone to emotionalism and that is visible in their writings etc abound.[28]

The other subject that has incorporated a gender perspective is again, a new subject, in China. Law. Chao Yunxin in her article uses a classic Marxist framework when she links women's subordination to the different modes of production and highlights how feudalism by denying women right to property and independence in law ensured their structural subordination. She points out how important it is for women's position to be strengthened through the enactment of legally enforceable rights. The article is also interesting in how it sees the evolution of laws related to women historically and points out the different categories of criminal law that pertained especially to women.[29]

Where a subject like politics is concerned, one sees the continued difficulty of explaining political participation as mere numbers of

26. *Ibid.*
27. *Ibid.*
28. Ravni Thakur, *Re Writing Gender: Women in Post Mao China,* Zed Books, 1996.
29. Zhao Yuanxin, "Law Viewpoint of Chinese Women", in DBWSMWR, *op.cit.* pp. 176-181.

women within the Party and in various leadership positions. While alluding to the practice of gender inequality at large, it merely mouths Party rhetoric when it uses phrases such as 'the necessity of correctly understanding the limitations of the historical stage of development'. Women's equality of participation in politics would naturally follow with the overall development of society. This of course is the classic Marxist paradigm that has always linked female subordination to the different stages of society and incapable of truly changing if this base remains unchanged.

One of the more interesting articles in the Reader looks at the participation of women in politics, especially the reasons behind their lower numbers within the Party. It focuses on notions of self-esteem and how women lack self-esteem and therefore do not have the courage to participate in politics. Guo Xueqian and Li Hiqing point out how increasing the participation of women in politics would require national commitment and strategic thinking.[30] They go on to stress that political participation by women should be a major responsibility of a socialist state. Currently only about twenty percent of Party membership is made of woman.[31]

Thus, overall, within a variety of subjects we see the emergence of a gender paradigm being incorporated with research methodologies and within the framing of research questions. The subject itself has generated a lot of debate on gender relations and also created enormous research data in different areas dealing specifically with the position of women. A critical perspective regarding the position of women is apparent in China and statistics prove the importance of gender sensitive policy planning. As Zheng Guichen points. In my country true gender equality still has a long way to go. The economic, political and social position of woman, generally lower than men.[32] Statistics dealing with the position of women in different fields consistently show them lagging behind men.

The return of more traditional ideologies of gender relations under the impact of global trends, have also led to the commoditisation

30. Guo Xueqian and Li Huiqing, "On Women's Participation in Politics", in *DBWSMWR, op.cit,* pp. 268-277.
31. *Iibid.*
32. Zheng Guizhen "Intellectual Women and Development", in DBWSMWR, *op.cit.* pp. 278-284.

of women through stereotype advertising and other media. This unfortunately is not accompanied by a woman's movement that accompanied the setting up of women's studies programmes in other countries. Discourse on gender, thus remains, limited to women's studies programmes and other intellectual urban settings. During interviews carried out with women students in Chengdu, they all stressed that despite greater equality, women were seen as the home makers and the men as the bread winners. Such ideas continue to ensure that women were discriminated against in the job market.

Thus, the complicated reality of contemporary China, its huge regional differences, make it necessary that more region specific studies be carried out. The woman's studies programmes in existence, are therefore, a welcome step in the right direction.

Comparisons with Western Women's Studies Programmes

Another areas of interest where women's studies in China is concerned is the comparison often made, in almost every article, about Western and China specific women's studies. The article by Chen Jiyan on "Theories of Women's Liberation" do point out what the right line on how this issue must be discussed.[33] It is revealing how China's idea of westernisation, democracy and in turn, feminism is defined by the need to differentiate itself the use of such categories in China as different from that in the West. While the attempt to create a China specific socialism was tied Mao's attempts to differ from Soviet style socialism, and the third world theory as part of his attempt to take over the leadership of the post-colonial world vis-à-vis Nehru, his attempt to take over world power shifted from competing with Britian in the 1950 to America by the late 1960's. The article points out that 'Feminism' is essentially a term prevalent in America and loaded with problems because of its politics of seeing the conflict between men and women as the basic conflict and ignoring other issues.[34] Here one can see that a socialist feminist programme is more attuned to China's ideological and recent history rather than liberal and radical feminist programmes that stress the need for women's independence from men, legally and sexually.

33. Chen Jiyan, "Reflections on the Theories of Women's Emancipation" in *DBWSMWR, op.cit.*, pp. 285-291.
34. *Ibid.*

The other important element of Woman's studies in China has been its attempts to draw upon an pan Asian identity and use that to differentiate itself from Western programmes. Du Fangjin presents the theoretical case for this. She writes in detail about the need to build a theoretical framework for woman's studies with a specific Asian content and perspective[35]. Theoretically, of course, this concept is old and part of our history of anti-colonial struggles. Even during the freedom movement there was contact with an idea and need to define a Pan-Asianism as against Western hegemony. Japan's breaking ranks during the Second World War, and it own history of violent colonial conquest in Asia, alas, dealt a hammer blow to this concept. From the Chinese perspective, this is also related to their overall attempt to create China as the mother culture for East Asia. The presence of large pockets of overseas Chinese and their influence in the economic sphere of countries such as Malaysia, Thailand and Indonesia and the economic inter-linkages between these areas also helps in China building closer ideological and issue based civil society ties with this region. Under Xi, we have seen a tightening of norms where gender discourse is concerned. The issues of sexual exploitation amongst party members and even the emergence of a major social media exposure of sexual exploitation at the highest echelons by China's international tennis star international tennis star, Peng Shuai and prior to that by other women, have been cleansed from social media sites and any attempt to promote "western feminism', academically and in public is severely curtailed. Like with the other social sciences, gender too has to be brought back under the ambit of Marxian analysis and linked to class not identity.

Conclusion

China is today a society undergoing rapid social and cultural changes. It has seen the quick expansion and growth or a consumer culture in urban areas, large scale migration from rural areas and also huge regional disparities. Along with this, the state has largely marketised its social services such as education and health, causing increasing hardship to people. All this has also led to the reemergence of a more traditional, Confucian, Chinese discourse on gender

35. Du Fangqin, "Developing Asian Women's Studies by Recognizing Difference and Similarity", in *DBWSMWR,* pp. 23-31.

relations. Gender equality, if we remember from the slogans of the Cultural Revolution like *Women Hold Up Half the Sky* and images of the woman from the Dazhai oil fields, woman were meant to and seen as able to perform all the tasks that men could. The excesses of the Cultural Revolution and its anarchy has put paid to all the symbols of that period. Nothing symbolizes this more than China's attempts to now create educational and other institutes in other countries that are called Confucian Institutes. This clear attempt to distance itself as the purveyor of communist ideology is a concerted attempt on China's part to say it is no longer Communist but a market economy that may be single party like Singapore and Taiwan once were.

The general discrediting of communist and socialist discourse in China, has also undermined its position on gender equality. In China, with the disbanding of the state sector, sixty percent of the laid off workers have been women. This has been coupled with the discourse of women should go back home and look after the family and let men be the bread winners. Another significant aspect of socialist rhetoric on gender relations is the protectionist discourse within which state support for female equality is couched. Women are constantly identified as those who need to be 'protected'. This is especially the case in China till the nineties. This essentially means women's rights are enshrined in the constitution as a gift from the Party not as something that women should have per se. This discourse of protectionism has been visible ever since the woman's question appeared as in the charters of social reform. The process is similar in India and China. All the stalwarts of the early reform period were men. During the socialist phase of the revolution all the women who emerged as leaders and intellectuals were consigned to head 'female tasks'.

In the final analysis, we know that gender relations is a complicated arena of social relations and gender equality cannot be reduced to reductive analysis such as the base-superstructure, false ideology that socialist discourse speaks of. In erstwhile socialist countries, women may have started participating in the labour market to a large degrees, but that did not change the structural or doxic nature of patriarchal discourse. Woman as the ultimate gift, the commodity par excellence as Marcel Mauss so brilliantly named it. We fight against that and yet we remain that. That is why women's studies programmes are so important. The setting up of women's studies programmes and the pushing of a gender perspective within policy planning and within other disciplines is therefore a welcome and necessary step forward in China. What China needs now is greater interaction within the international movement of women and greater academic exchanges with other countries. We need to continue our fight for equality and we need to ensure that it is not limited to small intellectual forums but reaches out to represent the discursive power of the Woman Question.

Chapter - VII

A Critical Nationalism: Youth in China

Introduction

The 'Me Generation', or the Eightiers, little Emperors, single children from middle class families, two sets of grand-parents and consumer crazy, have been the superficial names that have been used to identify contemporary Chinese youth. They were born into a changed China, a China free of the radical egalitarian agenda of Mao Zedong and his Cultural Revolution and a common Communist paradise. They have grown up in the post-1978 world, in a China where wealth and success are acceptable career goals. Where in fact, careers proliferate as China not only embraces the world with a vengeance it also assumes to lead it.

The massive shift from a socialist, centralised system to a 'state capitalist' economy in China has initiated major changes in the relationship that individuals have with the state. A centralised communist state meant the complete vertical integration of society with the state allocating all resources, including those of education and jobs. The personal was eroded at all levels, those of love, of marriage, parenthood and even self identity. The category 'comrade' subsumed the individual and the category class defined one's identity and status. The erstwhile structure of vertical dependency, to use Kornai's term, that characterised most Stalinist states in East Europe and China, also meant that the idea of the 'individual' or the category of individual subjectivity, was per force subsumed under the goals of socialist state building. For China's intellectual history, it meant that a project begun in the May Fourth Movement of 1919, remained an unfinished project through the hard years of Mao's ideological imperatives.

The first student movement in China, called the May Fourth Movement of 1919, was a revolt against the old traditional Confucian culture that had ossified and left China behind in a world governed by Science and Rationality. The slogans of this period were *Mr. Dai* and *Mr. Sai* or Mr. Democracy and Mr. Science. Their fight was both nationalist in nature and against the old order. Mao Zedong himself was the product of this period, having been a librarian at the Beijing University, and then a founding member of the Communist Party in 1922. The call given by intellectuals like Chen Tuxiu, who went onto become the Communist Party's first General Secretary, in his magazine the New Youth (*Xin Qingnian*), was to create a new Chinese society and a new man. May 1919 was the result of China's first engagement with Western ideas and a critical inward search for a Chinese answer to solve its social and economic problems.

Even Communist China that under Mao repudiated all traditional structures and organisations, had Mao put his faith in youth when he fell back on their idealism and radicalism to push his own agenda forward against his Party rivals during the Cultural Revolution. His storm troopers, the Red Guards, swore on his Red Book to attack the old guard and those who were identified as representing old values and Confucian or traditional ideology. Their goal too was to create a new 'Chinese'. A post-1978 China also witnessed student activism with tragic consequences at Tian Anmen in 1989. They too demanded a complete over throw of the old system and an end to a single party communist state. They asked for a fifth modernisation, democracy. Their hopes and enthusiasm was belied by the tanks that ran over the square under the orders of the CCP leadership.

The opening of China to the world and the growing interaction amongst Chinese youth with other cultures and political systems, access to modern technology and the internet revolution since the nineties, is perhaps the second engagement with the West. Once again, it has changed the way youth today relates to both the state and society. The choices that education offers those who can access it is enormous. Globalisation has also created global options. And today, it is access to education that determines the path forward for youth.

It is these changes that I have sought to examine here. This chapter is based on interviews that I carried out with students in Sichuan and Beijing University, in November 2005. The purpose of this field work, was to examine the emergence of a middle class in

China and university youth, belong to this class and aspire to belong to this class. This chapter highlights some generalised opinions about youth in China and identifies the two major trends that can be seen. One is the growing sense of individualism, and the second, the rise of nationalism. Although the focus is on elite college graduates, I have also included information about working class youths.

The next section will look at the changes in the Education sector in China before examining its student population.

The Privitisation of Education

The Chinese government introduced a new education policy in 1995. This was designed to streamline China's higher education system to suit the needs of the new economic policy that had by the late eighties moved away from restructuring agriculture to restructuring urban industry. The need was felt to expand the education base to include new specialisations and new departments away from the emphasis on politics that had previously dominated education. Chief and most popular amongst these new subjects introduced are the faculties of business management and law. New emphasis has also been placed on economics and international relations and area studies are being given increasing importance. The changes were also designed to overturn the State's paying for free education for the masses. Education, like health was meant to have consumers pay for it instead of being a public good as it was earlier. While in the earlier system, central investment in education stood at 51%, provinces at 20% and users at the grass roots ended up sharing 29 percent.

According to the *China Economic Times* (18-10-2005, p. 5), total investment by the center stands at only 2 percent, provinces at 11 percent, counties at 9 percent and villages and small towns (xiang/zhen) at 78 percent. Thus, the onus on lower units to ensure that the target of nine years education is met, is enormous and shows especially in poorer districts. Although these figures are essentially for primary and secondary education, never the less they show how education is no longer seen as a direct responsibility of the State. The most significant change in China's educational system was the introduction of fees at all levels of schooling, from primary to university. Parents I spoke with in Beijing and in Sichuan pointed out that 10,000 yuan is the minimum amount a middle income family spends on schooling per annum and this can rise with extras for extra activities thrown in.

The fee structure in Sichuan University (giving a general picture) is as follows for basic courses. It is higher for medical, science, art and film institutes because of the students being required to pay for all materials used.

Fee Structure (2005) at Sichuan University

BA courses liberal and science	
(*Benke xuesheng three year course*)	4000 yuan p/a
Boarding	1000 yuan
Food and living	4000 yuan
	(as told by students and staff).
MA students (*yanjiusheng* four yrs)	8000 yuan

The MA courses are being restructured and will now last only three years. Other costs are the same. The latest figures for 2018 show University fees in premier tier universities such as Beijing and Shanghai now stand at 23,000 per year (2,768 $). All other costs would have risen accordingly.

Further, at the BA level no scholarships are available although poor students can avail bank loans but this in turn depends on the subject of study and payback guarantees provided. Normally, the 0.5% interest loan is expected to be paid back within three years.

At the MA level, scholarships are available but these are based on merit rather than economic need. These structural changes have ensured that access to the higher levels of education are becoming restricted to a certain monetary capacity. This, in turn, has changed the overall student community, turning it into a middle-upper class domain. Many students from well off families now travel abroad for higher education. This must be kept in mind when we speak of youth in universities today.

In the next section, I am going to speak of the hopes and aspirations of students, and point out how, their options today show a growing sense of individual identity rather than a sense of collective comradeship, the hall mark of Mao's China.

Security, Status and Power

Not surprisingly, ideas of their future included jobs, which in their minds, provided both social status and a sense of security. Here of course their own specialisations influenced their decisions. All of them hoped to start with a basic salary of above 3000 yuan. This was seen as the lowest they would like to start with and essential if one was to approach a middle income or middle class status. The variation in specialisation also marked what they thought they would achieve. A student doing an MA in software programming was sure his starting salary would be above 7000 yuan per month.

I was however told that given the rise in educated unemployed in China today, they may have to settle at lower levels, especially if they failed to secure government jobs. Finding a job after graduation is indeed a real tension especially if one looks at recent statistics on the subject. Today urban employment in China stands at roughly 4% and half those graduating do not immediately find jobs. Again this does not include under employment – a major complaint amongst especially BA level students. According to Chinese statistics amongst ordinary, that is BA graduates, only 73 percent found jobs while amongst MA students 84 percent found jobs. Thus, a university degree is not a guarantee of employment. It is even less a guarantee that they will find the kind of jobs that they would like to have. The number one choice of the majority of my sample was government jobs, the second preference was for private sector jobs where through hard work one could rise to a managerial position and the third for university jobs.

All the students that I interviewed pointed out how social status and power was still not necessarily tied to money earned. In fact their identification of themselves as intellectuals was in itself symbolic of how status is closely linked to symbolic capital. The old idea and respect of intellectuals in China still resides and knowledge is still the goal of all Chinese, rich or poor. A very rich entrepreneur was still seen as lower in terms of social prestige than what are recognised as middle class professions. In terms of social status and in terms of power senior party functionaries were universally seen as possessing the highest of both. This was interestingly enough followed by managers of enterprises at number two and university professors at number three.

Other liberal university professions like doctors, lawyers and finally private entrepreneurs.

Thus, one notices, a decided conservatism amongst Chinese students who put a sense of long term security personal security at a higher premium than a fat cat salary. The sinecure of a safe government job and the ultimate ambition of being senior leader, showed both the way society evaluates social status and also how state power in China remains of great import. This should not be seen as an aberration. In fact the linkages between intellectuals and the State goes back to China's ancient examination system that led to the emergence of a class of litarati as administrators and imperial officers. Further, the deliberate promotion of Confucianism and Confucian values has again revalidated the status of the intellectual class.

Challenges Facing China

Although, I did not ask any directly political questions, I was able to approach the subject by asking students what they felt about China today and what they identified as the main problems that China still faced. Except for one student who was already a party member, none of the students showed any interest in politics. They said that China was a 'non-political' society. However, this was one issue where they did not all display the uniformity that they did on other issues. Simple things like would you define China as a socialist or a capitalist society, I got varied answers and the clue really lay in their definitions. The majority thought China was socialist in that it was led by the Communist Party and officially defined itself as a socialist country. One even went on to say instead of a 'Chinese specific socialism', China society should be seen as 'China specific capitalism' or *Zhonguo teshu de ziben zhuyi*. I want to point out some of the more interesting discussions that I had on this subject. Since these were one to one conversations, had outside the library, in my room, two students even asked me whether my room was tapped, showing once again the real danger and fear that exists if one is too critical of the Party or the lack of democracy.

The students identified three main problems facing China. The first, and this was interestingly brought up by the majority of men, less by the women students. More democracy or *gengduo de minzhuhua*. By this they meant not just the freedom of expression but the right to get away from appealing to party contacts for good jobs, good openings in business and above all allowing 'merit' to really find a place in Chinese society. Thus, more democracy was definitely an appeal to get away from the overpowering control that the Party still exercises. I had the good fortune to meet one female student who was a party member with both her parents who were also party members. The father cynically pointed out that the young had no idea of the kind of freedom that they now enjoy since they never suffered under the daily monitoring that his generation had faced.

The students cynicism about the Party was also brought out by their attitude to the compulsory 'political class', or *zhengzhi ke* that they are accepted to attend from primary school right through their BA. This has to be passed before they can go on to the next year. 28 of the fifty interviewed felt that this class was really unnecessary because every thing that was taught in the class was the opposite of what real life was. *Dou she huashuo.* Its all lies one told me. This class at the primary level consists of morality stories built around communist heroes and by the BA level they are accepted to have read their basic Marx, Engels and Mao. They also have to be familiar with Deng's work and the theory of three represents put out by Jiang Zimin. Under Xi Jinping, these classes have been strengthened and further promoted. Marxism was seen as being in disjunction with reality. Thus, the ideological propaganda of the Party or its claim to represent the masses is seen as hollow. "It is a dog eat dog world", said one final year male student "and the Party is the Tiger".

The Party's or the State's control was also seen as closely linked to corruption within the country. This was raised by both sexes and was in turn linked to the lack of democracy in decision making. I was told how good journalists were known by word of mouth and wrote on blogs which they constantly changed and how news of a good article on the internet was quickly passed around by sms. Now that China will also be monitoring sms's one fears an increased climate of tension in universities.

The main areas of corruption pointed out were the way money was wasted on unnecessary pomp and also how rather than money as such gift giving was the norm where senior cadres were presented with expensive gifts. This problem was clearly identified by a private entrepreneur who ran internet advertising from a posh group of flats in central Chengdu. I was treated to a gift since he intends coming to India!! Corruption also takes on the famous inspector raj that we are familiar with in India. This can be power, electricity and where restaurants are concerned health inspectors. It seems that the lower ranks are given money while the higher lot are entertained. But for the students, corruption took form in the kind of privileges that govt. servants enjoyed and how almost all the new rich of the nineties were offspring of Party members and their kin.

A young boy of 23 who ran a café in a hotel full of foreign students, had both parents in the Party and his father was a senior cadre in Chengdu. He made 12 thousand yuan on an average each year and had already traveled a lot in China. He was simultaneously studying Management at Chengdu University. A Party I attended at his café had students from China, Nepal, Palestine, America, England and of course, Hongkong. A Party that belonged to any university periphery anywhere in the world.

The third and final issue that all the students brought out was the increasing income and social disparities that exist in China today. Two of the students had accompanied me on my interviews with construction workers who came from out of Chengdu and only spoke the Sichuan dialect. Their shock and embarrassment was visible when they saw the way the workers lived. All of them commented on how this could be a destabilising force, especially in rural areas. Where inequalities were concerned, all the students thought that this phenomenon was now increasing visible in urban areas was leading to situation that could lead to trouble. They pointed out that life was hard for the poor in the city and the government though making the right statements, did little to help. They all felt that the government must control its officials better.

Here again, I had an interesting discussion with my group in Beijing University. They thought that the maximum corruption in rural areas and a source of conflict in urban areas was the way people's houses and land had been earmarked for change of status and the compensation paid was far less than they were told since most of it was being pocketed. One female student pointed out the example of a specific area in Beijing, the north-east where this had occurred. One student from Anhui province, a poor peasant area pointed out that land from peasants had also been taken in similar circumstances.

Here one also sees the continuous importance of the Party where both power and social status is concerned. It is still the effective ruler and distributor of power and has the ability to pull the plug anytime that it wishes. The desire of students to join the Party was also linked to this real and effective power that the Party continues to enjoy. Middle class status may allow for the freedom to consume, travel and lead comfortable lives but it still does not allow them access to positions of real status unless they are members of the Party themselves.

A Middle Class Nationalism

Yet despite the growing criticism of the problems and the Party, where China's place in the world was concerned, nationalism was the dominant feeling. Since 1989, the CCP has carried out concerted propaganda to promote a sense on national identity based on anti-western and national pride in China's achievements and current economic and international status. This Chinese, and often, Han nationalism, is visible most openly in the blogosphere, now so popular in China. Student opinion has attacked the world for interfering in Tibet and for attempts to preach human rights to China. The sentiment of Tian Anmen seems to have dissipated in a surge of nationalism. Anti-Japanese sentiment forms the basis for a resurgent nationalism, being pushed through media and in history writing. Since I was from India, questions about Tibet and the "splittism" of the Dalai Lama was also raised and the Dalai Lama roundly criticized by all the students I spoke with. Anybody challenging the territorial integrity of China, including Taiwan, was a no go area. Several of them felt that love for the nation or *aiguo zhuyi* must not be equated with love for the Party. They felt that they criticized the Party or were pointing out its shortcomings because they felt it was harming the nation. This is an important distinction because the Chinese Communist Party has always equated nationalism with communism and with itself as the champion of both. This is also part of the tradition of Chinese intelligentsia that has had scholars and Confucian literati who have petitioned and criticized Emperors if they felt they were deviating from their duty to the nation. It was also interesting to note that while this nationalism is suffused with pride and a feeling that China is no longer a victim but a leader, it is also filled with a sense of commitment to solving the current problems of China.

Finally, I asked the students who they identified as the best leader China had had. Two of the fifty said Mao Zedong. 18 identified Zhou Enlai. 4 identified Zhu Rongji but they were students of economics. And the rest of course identified Deng Xiaoping. When asked to give their reasons, they said Mao was turned into a god, but he made so many mistakes. Zhou was seen as epitomizing nationalism. The students all felt that he had sacrificed his whole life for the nation and had even refused to have children. Deng Xiaoping was revered as the realist who unleashed China's potential and turned China into a prosperous country that could now hold up its head in the corridors of world power.

Conclusion

University students seems to form a bridge of continuity with this idea of a great China that has always haunted the Chinese intelligentsia. Today, we see amongst Chinese university students, a reawakened Chinese nationalism, linked to its old histories, instead of linked to the last sixty years of Communism. The CCP too, has allowed expression of nationalism in public, against Japan, against the bombing of the Chinese consulate in erstwhile Yugoslavia by the American forces. They have also tried to use it as a bargaining chip with the students, to direct their activism and passions away from questioning the iron fist of the CCP or of questioning the growing disparities in their own society.

One sees two major shifts in the way Chinese youth today see themselves. The most important is their criticism of the problems currently faced by China. The second is a growing sense of nationalism that will not tolerate criticism of China and is rapidly creating an atmosphere that borders on the xenophobia. Yet one notices that Chinese youth remain committed to the idea of a great China and cannot be described merely as spoilt children of the eighties. Instead they form the cohort of the emerging middle class (es) in China.

The idea of the middle class, its social status, its access to leisure, and of course that basic income that allows all this. It is this idea that dominates the lives of students in China. And they will have access to all of this or at least the majority will. In conclusion it was obvious to me that China is now dominated by middle class values that include self interest and yes that desire for stability and pride on behalf of the nation. When asked for notions of civil society, not really part of my questionnaire but asked at random to those who gave more interesting replies in terms of democracy and the role of the Party, I was told that in China there are no options. There is only one party and despite all its shortcomings, the Party was seen as providing stability. What even the young fear most is 'chaos' *(luan).*

The middle classes therefore draw their legitimacy in China from the State and the Party and it is not surprising that the two are closely linked and that the majority of students hope to enter the state administrative sectors, especially the central administrative system that is equivalent to our IAS and has an exam after which depending on the states needs, 4000 students are chosen annually based on exam results. Here Party membership is an important criteria as was pointed out by all the students.

At the theoretical level, I found two main questions that arise. One, the making of a group consciousness and network based or *guanxiwang* connections that operate in the spread of influence and status in China. Secondly, it also shows that class alone cannot help understand social distinction and its practice. Here the notion of symbolic value and cultural capital becomes extremely important. The middle class is, to paraphrase E.P Thompson, is still in the making in China. My paper has in fact really attempted to provide an understanding of the manner in which the new Chinese middle class is being created and how its self identifications work amongst those who are the most likely to become its members, its elite student population. This making of group consciousness is new in China because of the way it was simplified to class and reduced to birth in Mao's time. Today, its self identification has shifted to the self and based on personal achievement not class or parent background alone.

Not surprisingly, most students came from firmly middle income families. Here the pre-dominance of those whose parents were members of the Communist Party was obvious. China has 81 million members in the Communist Party. This goes once again to show the continuing importance of how membership of the Party ensures, not just access to education and other form of social capital, it also shows how the middle class itself is largely associated with the Party. The desire of the students to join the Party as a means of social climbing was also significant. This has always been the case in China as several scholars both western and Chinese have often commented. However, I was told by a Prof. of Sociology at Beijing that this would not necessary be the case in Southern China, especially areas where money making and successful entrepreneurs has created an entirely different affluent class.

While the university students gave a great deal of importance to lifestyle and ideas of freedom and money, the non-university youth was only interested in making and finding ways to make money. Interestingly, this group also emphasized the need to depend on oneself and not on the government. They had less faith in the government in being able to provide for them. One thing that both groups had in common, was the acceptance that having contacts with those within the Party, was crucial to set up businesses and helped in finding a good job.

What this will mean for social change and whether civil society will emerge in China as separate from the Party and be able to effectively demand social change remains speculative. China has critical intellectuals who question the over importance of China's economy on growth and too little on social welfare.

The middle classes have benefited the most from government economic reform and want the stability, consumption patterns and travel even if ruthlessly provided by the Communist Party to continue. They have vested interest in maintaining the status quo. I did ask the students who came from rural areas about elections in their villages, I was told that the candidates are still selected from the Party and approved by them. Secondly, successful peasants are given priority to stand for elections and thus, administrative control. Notions of civil society and democracy, are of course, argued away as western and unsuitable to Chinese culture. Instead, many, not the students but other intellectuals that I spoke with, saw China as reverting to older Confucian value systems where nationalism has always meant the right to criticize bad practices but still avow loyalty to the Emperor – in this case the Party.

The youth of China straddle a complicated world. They live in a China where the opportunities before them to better their own lives were unimaginable for their parents and grandparents. Yet, like youth, the world over, their goals and aspirations combine a desire for economic betterment and status with a strong nationalist sentiment that puts the overall development and rise of China as more important than the fulfillment of personal ambitions. While membership of the Party remains a crucial guarantee of status, wealth and secure jobs count as equally important. The one idea that Chinese youth must not aspire to is Democracy, the ever failing dream of Chinese youth, from the May Fourth to Hong Kong in 2020.

Conclusion

Challenges Before Xi Jinping

Xi Jinping is undoubtedly one of the most powerful leaders in the world today. He rules over a population of more than one billion, has the second largest economy in the world and its trade links and investments span the globe. It also has considerable hard power at its disposal. It has a rapidly expanding blue water navy, huge investments in the fields of cyber informatics and robotics, a robust and highly successful space programme that augments its streamlined military. It also has an advanced industrial base and a literate population. Further, it now leads the world in registering scientific patents and publications in credited scientific journals. Thus, without a doubt, China under Xi Jinping is a country backed by considerable comprehensive national power, that is economic, military and scientific. China has arrived at achieving its goals of avenging a century of humiliation as the Chinese Communist party designated the last century. Today China considers itself capable of commanding and demanding respect and even subservience. And recently, it has been doing so rather aggressively. It is a **Fuqiang Guo**, a rich and strong nation.

So what is China's future under Xi Jinping? Will it actually become the world superpower and challenge the USA for supremacy and create a new Pax China, based on a model considerably different from that which has sustained the world order since the second world war? Does its rise to power to entail exporting its communist authoritarian model that has tried to shout down any criticism of China by arresting international journalists, boycotting commodities and threatening to cancel trade orders? These are legitimate questions to ask as we see China's competition with the USA take on a more strident edge.

In this book, we have tried to show not just the strengths of China under Xi Jinping, but also the specific ideological and organisational changes that Xi Jinping has enforced over the past eight years of his rule. These have been designed to bolster Xi Jinping's own indisputable leadership and to showcase China as a new power that can challenge the old western world order. In every way, Xi has concentrated all power in his own position. We see a Xi cult now in full play, his portraits, his thoughts, plastered across billboards in China. Xi is not one amongst equals, he is definitely and far above them, his thought enshrined in the Constitution, elevating him to the same stature as Mao Zedong, fifty years before him.

For the first time since Mao Zedong, China is once again, being brought under extensive Party control through modern means of surveillance and the systematic elimination of any dissenting voices. Any signs of independent academic discourse have also been muzzled. Reinforcement of the intellectual superiority of Marxist methodologies as against liberal intellectual traditions that stress human rights, individual rights and freedom of expression, is mandatory in all academic courses. More importantly, frameworks that encourage innovation and transformation, are now once again being subsumed under ideological rigidity. "Red and Expert", the slogan of the Maoist times seems back in vogue. Any access to information is strictly controlled through the heavily monitored and a firewalled internet. It is generally accepted that China has more than 100,000 young people employed only to monitor the net and pull down any content that is in any way critical of the Communist Party and especially Xi. Words such as Democracy, Tian Anmen were already banned on the net even before the time of Xi Jinping, but today the lexicon of banned words has expanded to include any mention of protests in Hong Kong, the incarceration of millions in Xinjiang and the forcible closure of Churches that are independent. Social media posts are systematically monitored and millions of cameras trace the movements of its 'good citizens' through the day. The relative openness of academic and media is now a thing of the past. Further, a growing and vibrant stream of investigative reportage by ordinary citizens who posted any wrong doing and especially conspicuous consumption by Party cadres, from expensive watches to luxurious banquets, are also no longer allowed, seen as demeaning the image of the Party.

In other words, any ideas challenging the role of the Communist party and its narrative of progress and power, and especially any criticism of Xi Jinping himself, must be quashed within campus centers, in the social media and other public spaces. Instead media waves are to be flooded with rigorous political education that stresses over and over again the importance, and the right of the party to rule. Xi has specifically targeted any deviation of ideological purity within the ranks of the party, calling it again a war or *douzheng*, a word he often uses to gear up the ranks for action. The very terminology is designed to give no quarter, casting those who oppose the Party, as at once anti-nationalist and playing into the hands of 'foreign powers'. Playing the nationalist card is the easiest way for authoritarian regimes to denigrate critics and even those who, while accepting the right of the communist party to continue ruling China, nevertheless feel justified in pointing out its shortcomings. This includes, writers, intellectuals, journalists and even the ordinary people, who feel that they have sacrificed for the country and have the right to be heard. Alas, Xi has chosen instead to quash even the softest criticism directed at the Party.

Apart from stressing the fundamental role of the Party in China's history of success, Xi has also stressed his own importance to this project for continued Chinese regeneration, the *China Dream*. He has abrogated the term limits set under Deng Xiaoping that limited the tenure of the President of the Country and has further strengthened his position through the creation of several working groups and committees all of whom he heads. Further, he heads the Military Commission and, has even brought under him, all local paramilitary forces. Xi now rules like an emperor within China, his thought enshrined in the Constitution and his personality cult well on the way to challenge the one that Mao had enjoyed. China is today a totalitarian country run by a dictatorial figure who sees himself as the only one capable of leading China to its legitimate place as a superpower in the 21st century. This is the goal of the Communist Party that Xi hopes to fulfill, thus securing his place in Chinese history.

Yet, as we have seen, China's future is not necessarily paved with gold. Xi faces several challenges both domestically and internationally. Many would argue that the very stress on the role of the Party, its goals and its history, in fact, point to the fragile legitimacy the Party actually enjoys. The façade of sustaining a "Communist Party and

Communist Ideology" in a capitalist society that does not provide its workers and peasants the right to protest, nor guarantees them any job security, is not easy. Nor is it easy to manage the real material interests that different regional and business lobbies exercise in China. This overarching concentration on ensuring the Party's legitimacy proves rather the fall in its legitimacy as China's domestic cleavages of income and prosperity re-shape social relations.

At the domestic level, his sharp turn against the relative ideological freedom enjoyed by the middle classes, and especially within academic spaces, and to a certain extent on social media platforms, has caught many by surprise. The growing control over access to and exposure to western thought and ideas, the curtailed freedom within campuses to have a frank discussion on the situation in China, have come as a shock to the intelligentsia and the student community. It has pushed dissent underground. The renewed focus on Marxism and ideological purity has meant that China will lose it growing research and analytic capacity in the field of the social sciences. A capacity, built over the last thirty years of relative freedom and openness. This will mean once again, unreliable and propagandist statistics that will impede systematic and truthful policy making and responses. Its interaction with western researchers, international university projects will all be joepardised under the circumstances.

China has also been witnessing growing working class and peasant protests in recent years. The incessant takeover of peasant lands to build infrastructure and housing, without fair compensation, has riled peasant communities over the country. Corruption and bribery have ensured that village areas are arbitrarily defined as development zones, allowing property developers to come in and acquire land at throw away prices, with little compensation given to the peasants whose fields have been acquired. It is estimated that more than 70 million peasants have lost their land in the last decade, and that number is expected to rise to above 100 million soon.

Not only is the peasant losing land but a diverse set of taxes, from road building to buying pigs can be extracted from the peasants. This, coupled with the removal of state sponsored health and education that was originally free, have seen peasants livelihoods shrink. Large scale youth migration to urban areas for work, has left some rural areas short of labour. We see a growing feminisation of rural labour and more and more rural households now consist of older grand-parents and young children, with both parents having migrated to cities to make a basic income. Despite the government introducing certain basic income schemes, the growing gap between rural and urban areas in China, makes Xi Jinping's grandiose dream of creating a middle class society more difficult.

China has also seen growing incidences of workers unrest in recent years. Workers have been agitating for their basic rights to fair wages and working hours, for insurance and accident coverage. They have led to the incarceration of many workers and even of students and intellectuals who may have come out in support of their struggles. The slow down of the Chinese economy and the trade push back from America, has created rising unemployment, especially at the lower end of manufacturing and mass production of cheap commodities. The current covid pandemic has heightened the threat to China's manufacturing sector even though it is the first economy to bounce back to normal. Although China's economy is the first to bounce back and Xi' emphasis on self reliance and a developing domestic market, bode well for it in the long term, the short term risks of disruptions, rising unemployment and a shrinking exports, remain.

China is decidedly different today than ten years ago when foreign researchers had the relative freedom to meet and exchange ideas with their Chinese colleagues. They also had far greater freedom to carry out research that challenged the overall narrative of growth and success that the Chinese Communist party has always touted as its legacy. It is through the work of Chinese scholars that we learnt of the increasing social disparities in China as the Iron Rice Bowl or the life time guarantees of the Maoist regime were withdrawn. It was through their work that we learnt of the transforming social structure of China as it reverted back to a more traditional class stratified society. We learnt about the increasing disparities amongst the regions of China and the plight of the migrant workers who eked out a living in China's sprawling manufacturing sector.

This emergence of two Chinas, one, of dominating sky scrapers and middle class consumption on the one hand, and on the other, the increasing disenfranchisement of the working and peasant classes, is the key challenge that Xi faces at the domestic level. Xi has tried to turn his anti-corruption campaign, as we have seen, into an instrument of Party reform. Yet, that may not be enough to assuage the general disenchantment with the Party at the popular level.

As explained in our discussion of social stratification, China has the highest gini coefficient in the world. If its social security figures are anything to go by, its millions of migrant workers and remote rural peasants still eke out a hand to mouth existence. Over the years, these inequalities, linked to contract labour, uncompensated land acquisitions by a state- developer nexus, unpaid wages of migrant workers and other such social injustices have prompted a constant round of protests across China. The Chinese government has now stopped giving out figures of protests but the last such figure and those by independent researchers record more than a hundred thousand protests annually of varying strength. Some, such as the protests of workers in southern China attracted world attention since they were championed by a new breed of young Marxist students who pointed out that a China claiming to be a Communist country must champion its workers and their rights. These students were later arrested and some remain missing. Protests have been met with increased authoritarian responses and discouraged strongly. Resort to draconian surveillance measures and extreme restriction of any expressions of dissent by arbitrary arrests, will only serve to push resentment deeper, creating a bubble that is waiting to burst. It is these realities that Xi Jinping has to manage even as he raises the expectations of his middle class supporters of a rich and powerful China.

China's economy has also shown a relative slowdown over the past few years from its amazing 9-10% GDP growth that it logged in over the last two decades to about 6%. While still impressive, this has meant problems at the levels of employment and where poverty alleviation and social security is concerned. China's economy also has a very high debt to GDP ratio of almost 48% in 2019, standing at nearly 5.40 trillion US dollars. This debt is largely been run up by regional governments that have invested heavily in the property development market, creating empty apartment blocks and towns in the middle of nowhere. This property bubble is one of the greatest dangers to China's economic stability since it is also the main avenue for people's savings. Thus, even though there is over capacity in the housing market, prices are still high in order to maintain the investment value of middle class savings. The economy would crash if property prices fell and middle class savings would be wiped out by any rationalisation. Thus, although houses remain out of reach of most buyers, they lie empty rather than being sold of cheaply. This model of constant investment in infrastructure and housing is unsustainable in the long run and poses a great danger to Xi Jinping's dream of having a largely middle class society in the near future.

Coupled with certain structural imbalances in the Chinese model of growth, such as the over dominance of the state sector and the constant control exercised over the private sector in China. China also lacks a robust domestic market, with the average Chinese still dependent on saving for a rainy day, and saving for investing in an artificially overpriced property market. Thus, China's consumption levels are low, its GDP dependent on exports and overseas consumers of cheap Chinese goods, a recipe that will need to be rapidly tweaked if China's large manufacturing sector and employment creator is to be sustained. This means encouraging domestic consumption, not easy for three basic reasons. One, as already explained, Chinese proclivity to invest in property and financial savings instruments instead of consumption. The emphasis on anti-corruption has meant a dampening down of conspicuous consumption by all government agencies, it has meant an end to expensive gift giving to bureaucrats for favours and, an end to hosting lavish banquets to entertain investor. And finally, domestic consumption will be hampered by the enormous income and wealth inequalities that now exist in China, where the bottom millions live on just enough to feed and clothe themselves. The latest statistics of the end of 2018, the number of people living below China's national poverty line of 2,300 yuan per year (in 2010 constant prices) is 16.6 million which translates to 1.7% of the population, with hopes of totally eradicating poverty by 2020. At the same time, however, income disparities have increased.

The danger to economic stability has been further exacerbated by growing US China trade tensions and the United States efforts to curtail China's unfair trade practices. This has not only affected China's manufacturing sector but hit hard at its growing and successful information technology sector, making it difficult for China to expand its markets and access new research and technology. China has seen push back from the European Union, from Australia and Canada. And now, more recently, by India and its ban on Chinese social media apps and games.

At the high end manufacturing sector too, the pushback against China's ambitions to dominate the new wave of 4G and other technologies, has already begun. China has been accused of stealing western technology, often through forced handover of technology by multinationals. The enormous state support given to their own technology firms to compete internationally, has also damaged China's reputation as a fair abider of free trade and WTO rules. The recent US call to boycott Huawei 4G networks in western alliance countries is in response to the calls by the Chinese state to demand that all their companies not only store all data in China but also hand over such data to the government when required. This has naturally raised security concerns amongst all democratic countries. The arrest of the Huawei heir in Canada has added further fuel to fire, with China and the US both making this a prestige issue. China has retaliated by arresting two Canadians in return, further upping the ante in a continuing tit for tat. The result of this war, however, is that several European countries, including Germany and Britain have pulled back from Huawei technology contracts in their countries.

China's aggressive military postures in the South China Sea, its abrogation of treaty obligations with Hong Kong, have forced Western countries to take note of the growing bellicosity and aggression of the Xi Jinping regime. And above all, its draconian incarceration of a million Uiguhur's in Xinjiang, amounting to what has been termed 'cultural genocide' by human rights organisations and by refugees scattered across the world, has finally brought scrutiny to Communist party rule in China. China's aggression against countries and groups that have raised issues of human rights and the rule of law, has further alienated world opinion, with many world leaders from the German Foreign ministry to Canadian Prime Minister Justin Trudeau announcing that China's "coercive" diplomacy will not be tolerated. Australian diplomats too have openly castigated China for its attempts to influence Australian politicians and control overseas Chinese students on the issues of Hong Kong and Xinjiang. Thus, the image of China has taken a severe beating internationally.

Growing public support for rights of the populations of Tibet and Xinjiang will also place further challenges for Xi in managing these already volatile border regions. As we have shown in our chapter on development in Tibet, China's claims of bringing development to these regions as a trade off for denying them ethnic and religious rights, appears hollow on closer analysis. The beneficiaries of the opening up Tibet and Xinjiang have been the Han Chinese who have migrated to these new regions under incentives promised by the national government in terms of lower taxes and easier investment loans for companies moving in from the more prosperous southern and coastal regions. Development Chinese style has in fact, led to greater marginalisation of the local populations of this region, pushing them further into villages, while towns and cities increasingly become centers of Han migration.

The efforts to counter China's aggressive economic and strategic diplomacy has led to concerned regional countries and the United States to come together in new security and strategic groupings, such as the QUAD, which has been elevated to a more formal footing with the meeting of its Foreign Ministers, held in Tokyo on the 7th October 2020. The United Stated openly touted this meeting as one between democracies determined to thwart China's authoritarian designs on the world systems. This grouping can, in the future, become a centre for pulling in other countries against an expanding Chinese foot print.

Thus, both domestically and internationally, Xi Jinping faces a number of serious threats to his rule, pushing him perhaps, into more aggressive stands against Taiwan and the world. This is indeed a recipe for disaster and may push the world into a second Cold War. The bi-partisan consensus amongst US politicians on a significant China threat, and the push back from European and other democracies does not augur well for the China Dream.

Xi Jinping's signature *One Belt One Road* project that hoped to build a China centric world by leveraging China's huge advantages and knowledge in infrastructure building and manufacturing, has also run into difficulties in recent years. More and more people are calling out China's debt based development paradigm. Here China loans countries huge amounts of funds to build infrastructure that they may not necessarily need. The contracts for building are then given to Chinese companies while the loans are taken by governments. Inability to pay loans have, in the past, led to China taking over sovereign territory, as it has done in the case of the Hanbantota port development in Sri Lanka. This debt trap diplomacy has seen a push back, not just in Malaysia but also in some African countries. It has also led to efforts by America, Japan and India to create alternative investment and development routes and strategies. Although President Trump pulled out of the Obama led TPP initiative, he has tried to put in place other institutions, to counter China's growing influence in the Indian Ocean Region. America has also increased its investments in Africa and is cooperating with its allies to create a wider constituency to check China's, and Xi Jinping's aims. The USA has, for the first time since 1972, specifically started targeting the Chinese Communist Party as the real villain, trying to draw a line between the CCP and the Chinese people. It is even considering sanctions against CCP members as a whole by denying them visas to study or visit the USA.

This weakness of Chinese soft power, its inability to build in genuine alliances across the world and its increasingly behaving like a colonial power with smaller African and Asian countries such as Cambodia, Pakistan and Laos, has further alienated international opinion. While calls to boycott the Winter Olympics led to Western State leaders not attending ceremonies, the call did find resonance across the social media. China only has satellite states in its orbit, the smaller ex-Soviet Republics of Central Asia, Pakistan, Myanmar and now Laos. China believes that its economic might and military power now allows it to create a China centric world, one that will not only impede the unilateral power exercised by the USA but will also allow China to slowly, but certainly, expand its overall sphere of influence. Several strategic thinkers in China analyse the USA as a declining power and China as the new, rising power that the world will have to contend with. They point to the internal discord of race, class and colour in the United States and the manner in which Trump has alienated many of his NATO allies, as the justification for their positions. Chinese thinkers believe their time has come to play a major, if not defining, role in international affairs.

Unfortunately for China, its internal and international problems have coincided with the world plague of the Covid virus that has seen more than a million people die across the world. The world, and especially, President Trump, have directly blamed China for this pandemic that has devastated the world economy and endangered people's lives. This has further exacerbated public opinion against China, leading to further calls to challenge China's growing international clout. A 2020 October Pew survey found that across several countries in western Europe and Asia, opinion had grown increasingly unfavourable for China and its investments.

Xi Jinping's management of domestic and international opprobrium will challenge his future term in office. He has to fulfill his vision of a Chinese Dream, continue to ensure that China's economy does not fall into problems as international trade regimes harden against China and China too uses trade to settle scores with countries such as Australia, Japan and South Korea. This has allowed Xi to give a nationalist colour to the criticism coming his way, whether for increasing internal authoritarianism or for an aggressive foreign policy conduct in the South China Seas and especially over Hong Kong and the incarceration of thousands of innocent Muslims in Xinjiang. This desire to deflect criticism may also lead China to inadvertent military confrontation within the South China Seas. Xi Jinping's military build up in South China, against Taiwan, is an ominous signal and may force the USA to come to Taiwan's aid if China does go ahead with its plan for militarily unifying Taiwan with the mainland. While China may be ready to challenge the USA, the results of any military confrontation cannot be guaranteed and could lead to unforeseen international consequences, further destabilising the world.

Thus, while Xi Jinping rules over a powerful and rich China, hubris and an overestimation of one's capabilities may spell danger in the immediate future. Many in China have argued for taking a more cautious line to all the emerging challenges, of still following in Deng Xiaoping's footsteps, and sheathing one's iron fist. But Xi has chosen to listen to those who push for an exercise of China's newly acquired military and economic might. This confrontational attitude may bring Xi nationalist support from within China but it will make it harder for China to achieve its stated goals of emerging as a new power center challenging the unilateral supremacy of the United States.

Appendix

Understanding India-China Relations

A Personal Perspective

The history of Indian foreign policy is closely associated with the 1962 war and the emergence of China as a continuing security threat. China's phenomenal rise through the past decades has enhanced this threat perception, once again brought to the fore during the 2017 Dokhlam standoff and, subsequently along the tenuous high altitudes of Ladakh since 2020, where for the first time since 1962, lives were lost on both sides. This latest series of confrontations has changed not only public perception of China within India, it has brought forth a strong diplomatic and strategic response from India, highlighting the fact that India too is not the India of 1962.

Since the famous handshake between Deng Xiaoping and Rajiv Gandhi in1988, the India China relationship entered a period of complex multifaceted engagement. India and China cooperate within several multilateral institutions such as BRICS and now the Shanghai Cooperation Organization (SCO). China is also our largest trading partner with bilateral trade crossing 100 billion dollars in 2021 although there is a strong trade deficit of 65 billion against India. Yet, as Indian Foreign Minister Subrahmanyam is quoted to have said, "We want good relations with China but good relations cannot be at the expense of National Interest" (4 Sept, 2022). For India, managing relations with China, thus remains the primary task. And that means developing a clear and objective understanding of China's foreign policy goals and its approach to India.

There can be no denying that since the reforms started in 1978, China has transformed beyond recognition. China has systematically used every device and opportunity to achieve its goals of emerging as a world power. It has proved that totalitarian Communist regimes can be very successful capitalist economies. It has also proved that for the West, profit trumps human rights! China has, especially under Xi Jinping, chosen to thumb its nose at the West and claim a 'Chinese style of governance', or what has been translated as the Beijing Consensus, where Democracy is seen as a chaotic system that does not suit China and where trade and economic growth should take precedence over any concerns for Democracy. China's economic integration with the world (China is the largest trading partner for most countries, especially Europe, USA and the BRICS 5), gives it huge heft and further, China is a member of the Security Council and today, plays a leading role in several UN organizations. It has emerged as the second largest economy in the world, at almost 13 trillion US$ and is counted as the largest economy in PPP terms. As a country, it is in a position to push its national interest forward in a comprehensive fashion within the international comity of nations.

Chinese National Interest and Nationalism

Since Deng Xiaoping's economic reforms of 1978 transformed the political economy of China, it has also transformed its sense of self as a nation, its relationship with its neighbors, and the world comity as a whole. The new nationalism and national goals that define China, see it as a confident world power that is equal to the USA and capable of defending its national interest. China's quest for the status of a world power, a strong nation state that commands respect from other world powers, has been achieved. The West may not like China but the US and allies have recognized it as the greatest challenge to the Pax Americana in place since the end of the 2nd World War. Taking ownership of this discourse of economic modernization and military strength, the Chinese Communist Party's vision of the nation, and especially that of Xi Jinping, is rooted in the following:

(1) A sense of recovering from100 years of humiliation at the hands of the West starting from the Opium Wars in 1839-43. This led to western domination and territorial concessions from China.

(2) Never allowing any one to put them in a position of subservience again. *Zhonguo* does not mean the center of the world (middle kingdom) but a China centric world.

(3) Owning the "modernization project", the belief in the progress offered by science and technology and now, the market economy.

(4) Revalidating the 'exceptionalism' of the Chinese civilization, its past achievements and cultural heritage.

(5) Combining modernization with Chinese culture in the Great Rejuvenation of the Nation.

(6) Creating the Communist party as the truest representative of China's rise and modernization, thus as the rightful leaders of China into the 21st century.

This discursive paradigm is really the raison d'etre that determines the priorities and positions of the Communist Party. This is also what underscores Chinese nationalism. For Xi and the leaders of the CCP, the people, the nation and the Party are one entity. The party cannot be separated from the people. Any attempts by the West to distinguish between the CCP and the Chinese people, is met with strong propaganda and offense internationally and draconian suppression internally. Any challenge to the CCP right to rule China or even share power has always led to a ruthless response. Under Xi Jinping, this unquestionable role of the CCP has been further strengthened and pushed again to the forefront.

The Stages of China's Foreign Policy

China's foreign policy reflects the changing self assessment that China has made of its goals and capabilities since 1978. Four broad stages can be identified according to the author and show a systematic and step by step chronological order, with each stage building on the previous. This shows China's long-term strategic planning and its intentions.

1. *Opening up to the World:* This was the initial phase under Deng Xiaoping, and he emphasized that his goal was internal development that needed a peaceful environment. This was really the golden period for solving border problems. China demarcated its borders with all its land contiguous neighbors, Russia and Mongolia for example. Only the boundary dispute with India remains.
2. *Peaceful Rise:* By the nineties, China's economic growth had surpassed all expectation and they had become the world's third largest economy. They were also the largest trading partner of most countries in the world and their investment reach spanned the globe, with Latin America and Africa becoming its favorite investment destinations. China had become a world power. During this period, China concentrated on building economic and political networks without challenging the status quo. It also funded massive military modernization over this period and invested in newer areas of R&D such as lasers, space and cyber systems. The US wars in Iraq were the catalyst for this annual double-digit growth and its concentration on R&D.
3. *Challenging the Status Quo*: This third phase, beginning in the second decade of the twentieth century, coincided with the last term of Hu Jintao and is being further strengthened by Xi Jinping. This leads to the period when China started exercising its CNP, a term that they first used, Comprehensive National Power. The Chinese

have followed the West in their quest for power. Understanding the importance of trade and a strong economy, while building up their hard power. It is going to use the defense of its trade interests and its man power in areas such as Africa, Venezuela to enforce and ask for the right to defend its investments. It is also going to use the international discourse on terrorism to substantiate its investments in its border regions because they coincide with race, ethnic and territorial divisions. Its push into South Asia is part of its peaceful and controlled peripheries strategy.

4. *Protecting Chinese Interests Across the Oceans:* Xi Jinping has put "Reunification" at the center of his strategic policy and as we have seen, the Taiwan issue has recently warranted unprecedented attention as both governments take more strident positions, forcing the USA too engage in several diplomatic confrontations with China, with the visit by House speaker Nancy Pelosi in August 2022 becoming a flashpoint. Clashes with India on the border a part of the same Reunification goal.

   China's maritime overtures are today taking center stage as it expands its own reach to the Pacific and the Indian Ocean. It is here that China is funneling huge investment. It is the South China Seas, and its disputes with Vietnam and Japan that have been in the news of late but its activities in the Indian Ocean are going to become increasingly important with Africa as its main sphere of influence lying at one end of the Indian Ocean. Its ports in Gawadaar, Myanmar and Sri Lanka are crucial for this. Its key goal here is to establish military outposts across the Indo-Pacific region though its "small island diplomacy", as it has shown with the Solomon Islands treaty in 2022. It is responding to the US challenge by extending its own reach into the US's back yard. Its military budget remains opaque but at the fifth session of the 13th People's Congress in March 2022, China announced a defense budget of 1.45 trillion yuan, a 7.5% increase from the previous year, making it a formidable military spender. This is coupled with the vociferous defense of Chinese positions within international forum, the Wolf Warrior diplomacy as it has been dubbed. This is the current phase, a confident and aggressive China ready to challenge the status quo in every field. This is the new nationalism.

II China's Goals vis-a-vis India

China does not see India as a direct rival except when it comes to claims over the Indian Ocean and any attempt by India to challenge China's boundary claims. In the immediate future, it sees its competition and challenge to its rise coming directly from the USA and its alliances. Its immediate aim is to curtail US presence in South East Asia and reclaim its historical position as the primary power in the region. While it does not see India as a threat to its integrity of Tibet any more since its military infrastructure development in Tibet far exceeds India's along its western borders, it does see India as part of a 'Contain China Policy' through alliances with the USA and Japan. China's main goal with regard to India is not to allow a strong strategic alliance to emerge between India, Japan and the USA. For, this purpose, it has systematically cultivated political and academic influence in India.

While the positions of Japan and the USA are clear, China thinks that India can be wooed away from the US camp. Given the previously strained US India ties under Nixon and Kissinger during the 1970's, there is still an anti US lobby in India. To this extent, they have gone out of their way to give India importance, as seen by their sending their Foreign Minister to Prime Minister Modi's swearing in ceremony. President Xi has personally invested in his bilateral relationship with Prime Minister Modi through the Wuhan and Ahmedabad and Mahaballipuram summits. They have also been cultivating Indian think tanks and other opinion makers, journalists, business lobbies etc through tour invitations to China and other outreach programmes. Their aims is to push the case for an 'Independent Foreign Policy' for India and emphasize the Panchsheel Accord between India and China as the only matrix for international relations. China also uses India's good relationship with Russia to help create positive opinion about an anti-Western common ground. Russia was instrumental in creating BRICS through the merger of RIC and IBSA.

Russia and China work along similar lines amongst decision-makers in India to push against a strong US-India partnership. This is going to become more important as the Ukraine war continues to play out, hardening position on every side. India's partnership in BRICS and now as a member in the SCO, have brought India closer to multilateral groupings that are Beijing centric. While this allows India a certain entrance into a China centric world, it also imposes on India a moral conundrum in aligning with any openly "contain China" groupings. This is indeed a challenge for India.

In the economic domain, China has great interest in the Indian economy both as an investment destination and as a market for their manufacturing products. They also hope to get a share of India's infrastructure development projects and would be happy to bid for roads and railway development and have consistently encouraged their regional heads to visit India and explore it as an investment destination.

However, they have greater interest in the new port investments in South Asia such as Hambantota in Sri Lanka and other Indian Ocean littoral states and in Gawadaar in Baluchistan. These effectively surround India on all sides and pose a great challenge to India's national security. Land based Chinese expansion in the region through its One Belt One Road Initiative with Pakistan is another major threat. India is in no position to challenge the highway that is currently being constructed from Kashgar in Xinjiang over the Kunjareb Pass, via Gilgit Baltistan to Gawadaar, and can only register diplomatic protests. This road is also closely linked to their strategy for Central Asia. Their relationship with Pakistan will remain the paramount lynchpin for any policy in South Asia. The One Belt One Road initiative, coming directly from President Xi Jinping, and one that India has naturally remained aloof from, will nevertheless, impact India's space for maneuverability in the region.

Possible Indian Strategies

The author would humbly venture to suggest a two-pronged approach in the management of the China conundrum. One would perhaps like to continue with the Rajiv Gandhi and Deng Xiaoping arrangement, where trade and economic interaction was separated from the security threats that remain unresolved. Territoriality is central to modern nation states and both India and China have to settle this boundary if any real partnership is to emerge between the two nations facing off across the Himalayas.

1. *Security Management:* India's immediate focus, especially after the incidents of May-June 2020, in the Ladakh region, should be the beefing up of its security infrastructure along both the Western and Eastern sectors. Any gaps in logistic and infrastructure needs of this sector must be immediately addressed keeping in mind China's massive infrastructure rail linkages to Tibet and other border regions, including a village right on the border with Arunachal. We also have to factor in China's access to India via Hanbantota, a huge security challenge for India and one that should never have been allowed to happen. While Gawadar is still in the making, Hanbantota now belongs to China for 100 years. This is a massive security challenge and Sri Lanka, despite the scandalous end to the Rajapaksa regime (2022), is in no position to change tack on this issue as demonstrated by the visit of a Chinese naval vessel to the port in the midst of a change of government in Sri Lanka this year. We need to consider the development of similar infrastructure and guard against any further developments in the region such as in the Maldives and Myanmar. At the same time, our islands of Car, Nicobar and the Andamans on one side and Lakshadweep on the other, could perhaps be rapidly enhanced as forward naval outposts.

A post-Dokhlam Strategy 2020

2020 has seen a cataclysmic change in Sino-Indian relations. The stand off that is currently taking place along the Western frontier of Indian's boundary with China, in the Dokhlam regions, has once again brought to the fore the centrality of the India-China boundary dispute, the longest boundary dispute in history. Although disengagement in the Gogra hot spring area is being reported by the media and government (Indian Express, 15 Oct, 2022), the situation remains far from normal.

The encounter occurred in the Galwan Valley, 60 kilometers north of the city of Ladakh. The incident started with China moving in three brigades (around 6000 troops) and the necessary supporting infrastructure to the eastern sector of Ladakh. It was reported that three brigades were moved to the Galwan valley and three into the Panggong Tse (lake) finger area region. What made this confrontation different from those of 2014 and 2017, was the multipronged military buildup on the Chinese side, including the Naku La in Sikkim, our eastern sector. China has recently also openly claimed large tracts of Arunachal Pradesh and disputed the right of India to change the status quo of Ladakh into a union territory.

There are several reasons why China has once again activated the border dispute. One is Pakistan and the opposition of both countries to the change in the status of Jammu and Kashmir, with the abrogation of article 370. This, and the constant pressure from their Pakistani partner to help build international pressure on India over the Kashmir issue, is another reason. Another important cause of this continued attempt to reshape the LAC in its favour is Xi Jinping's own emphasis on the Grand Unity of China, a goal of the Communist Party since 1950 and its claims to all of erstwhile Tibet and Taiwan. China will always claim Arunachal, both because it lies at the fertile end of the Tibetan plateau, with enormous water resources that China needs to power its ever expanding industrial needs, and also because it keeps the pressure on India along all fronts. China has shown disregard for the 2005 accord that was signed between the two countries that agreed populated areas would not be destabilized.

India has responded well to the 2020 standoff with China, holding its ground and countering China by accelerating its own military buildup along the contested border. It has successfully faced off China and held several bilateral talks, both at the military commanders levels and at the Foreign Minister' levels. The National Security Advisors of both countries have also met to try and diffuse the tension (June-October 2022).

However, the most significant response from India has been the acceptance of the QUAD, the group of four, made up of Australia, America, Japan and India. The beginning of this grouping goes back to the 2004 December Tsunami, when the navies of all four countries responded to the disaster. India's huge maritime boundary, its naval range and naval capability, were for the first time, showcased in the Indian Ocean Region. Since then, several informal meetings, designed as a casual security dialogue on the strategies necessary to ensure a Free and Open Indian Ocean Region, have been held. The main architect behind the idea had been the Japanese Prime Minister, the late Shinzo Abe, who first mooted the concept in 2007. However, due to Chinese pressure, both India and Australia initially demurred. Again, in 2012, Prime Minister Abe floated the Democratic Security Diamond, involving the QUAD countries, once again to guarantee the freedom of the commons in the IOR region. However, it was in November 2017, that a degree of formalization was bestowed on the QUAD by all four countries accepting the necessity to safeguard the freedom of the seas and keep it free of "any influence".

Although China was not directly cited, the inference is clear to all, including China. China has already dubbed this another "contain China strategy", being orchestrated by the USA. In recent years, each country has been facing its own set of problems with China. Australia has objected to Chinese interference in its politics, and with threatening Australian citizen's in China. Australian journalists and businessmen have even been incarcerated on charges of harming national security. Japan has been facing constant Chinese aggression in the South China Seas, and India is faced with the aggressive contours of Chinese policy in its border regions. This growing Chinese aggression, and the 2020 border standoff between India and China through the summer, has also hardened India's public and political stands against China.

The 2020 *Foreign Affairs Security Dialogue*, a meeting of QUAD Foreign Ministers, under the aegis of the QUAD has, for the first time, given this grouping the imprimatur of complete State legitimacy. This is the right way forward and India should not hesitate to further its association with the QUAD in terms of security and intelligence sharing. It must also further activate its maritime cooperation and naval exercises with these countries to give greater momentum and traction to this emerging security architecture. The QUAD has the potential to emerge as the fulcrum of a security architecture that can in the future, include as partners other Democratic countries in the region and thus provide an emphatic answer to China's growing aggression in the region. While each country will have to balance its own economic interests as it deals with China, alliances of a security nature may become necessary as both Xi Jinping and China stride across the globe to fulfill the China Dream.

The United States push back against China has also helped strengthen bilateral military exchanges and confidence building between the USA and India. We have now signed on to three agreements with the United States that allow us a partnership in information sharing, especially through GPS and satellite systems and we have agreed to allow refueling and docking for US naval ships on our naval bases. A strong bilateral strategic relationship with the USA and within the QUAD should allow India to balance the growing asymmetry between India and China. It may also allow India with a bargaining chip against China's growing clout in South Asia.

2. *Trade and Multilateral Cooperation:* While augmenting her security apparatus at every level to combat a rapidly advancing technologically up-to-date Chinese security structure, the author would like to argue that India must, in contrast, open its doors wider to trade with China. Here the advantage lies with India since we have a developed and robust domestic market and should seek to attract labor intensive manufacturing from China. This will not only bring in skilling of our work force but also allow us to increase our share of the export market in this sector. There is no harm in drawing in Chinese investment, especially in the manufacturing sectors such as textiles and plastics. This will ensure a degree of leverage on India's side, as has been shown by the ban on Chinese internet apps and the consequent financial costs to China.

India can take advantage of the investment funds at the disposal of China's private sector. The idea of a special Chinese investment Park is one such idea that would also allow regulation of Chinese business. India could benefit and take advantage of China's need for low labour cost production as its own labour costs rise. China is the only country from where we will get labour intensive industry, a necessity for India, given its population, low education and HDI indicators. China is already outsourcing to Bangladesh and Sri Lanka in the textile sector and India must attempt to enter this loop to our own advantage. In internal discourse, India is discussed as a destination because of its own needs, its large growing consumer base and because SE Asia is already saturated with Chinese investment. China's investments in the non- security sector infrastructure development too should be considered since they are truly good with largescale infrastructure development and have very economical rates. Of course, labour contracts and reciprocal Indian investment in China's service sectors should be effectively bargained for. India would not need to take loans from China for this kind of investment and therefore have no fear of being cornered like smaller economies. Increasing western sanctions have crimped China's expansion and India can bargain from a position of strength over economic relations. We should also raise the unfair trade balance that currently exists between the two countries. But the author feels that India is strong enough to allow China's private sector into key areas without feeling threatened. However, the recent military and political distrust has impacted all levels of interaction and regaining the older bonhomie in the economic sector will take time.

In terms of its own forward geo-economic strategies, we could increase economic and strategic presence in the near neighborhood. China's expanding footprints in South Asia and South East Asia should be of great concern to India, especially with regard to Nepal and Sri Lanka in South Asia and Myanmar and Cambodia in South East Asia. There is widespread consensus amongst political and policy circles that India must enhance its own connectivity with the region through rail and expanding road networks. Indian outreach to Sri Lanka during its recent economic and political crisis of 2022 has been exemplary. The Lankan economy is already facing a crisis brought on by its loan repayments to China. India must enhance popular perception in Lanka about its support for them by augmenting greater connectivity between the two countries. At the same time, the perils of being economically dependent on China must be brought home forcefully, to other regional partners.

Greater Use of Indian Soft Power

India can and should emphasize its democratic credentials. We are the only 'Third World Country' that has been democratic since Independence. It stands in contrast to China as an alternative Asian political and cultural trope. Our links to our neighborhood are informed by culture, language and shared histories. We need perhaps to reclaim this syncretic Asian Heritage. India's Look East Policy has suffered from its neglect of South East Asia i.e Vietnam, Laos, Cambodia, Thailand, Burma. During recent travels and interactions with policy- makers in this region, the author discovered that India would be a welcome investor and service provider and is seen as the only logical partner for democratic forces in the region. Here the situation in Myanmar requires greater support for the democratic process and for its now incarcerated leader, Aung San Suu Kyi. Our respect for liberty, plurality of religion and opinion and for the due process of law is what has distinguished us from China in the past and it must continue to do so. China's lack of soft power despite attempts to buy into international media, is a great handicap and India's strength.

India can also make huge education sector investments in this region. During the 60s and 70s India was a premier destination for South Asian students in search of quality and affordable education. We must once again leverage our huge human resources to become an attractive university destination. At the same time, relearn and put in place joint research projects on India and South East Asia and put in place long term projects of reclamation and renovation of common cultural sites in Vietnam, Cambodia and Myanmar and Thailand. We are already doing so, but these activities must generate more publicity and enhance mutual ties.

Nalanda University could play a major role in this cultural reclamation and interaction. It could become a center of excellence for the study of ancient Indian and South East Asian and East Asian interactions. We could carry out research on languages like Pali, Brahmi and Sanskrit and its uses and interface in our near region. China is creating a Buddhist network, starting with Lumbini and the training of monks and nuns to spread Buddhism as one aspect of its soft power out reach. India too must reclaim its composite cultural linkages with East Asia and its cultural heritage, especially the best of the syncretic Indo- Buddhist pluralist heritage that still resonates in South East and East Asia.

Another cultural sector that enjoys huge popularity across the world, and especially in Central and South Asia is our film industry. Indian film stars have massive fan followings and the film industry and film stars can play a very positive role in furthering the soft power cultural heritage of India. The industry can also shoot films in these regions and work on joint projects. The author has been in remote parts of China and South East Asia and been treated to India film songs and names of film stars from Nargis and Raj Kapoor amongst the older generations and to Amitabh Bachchan, Salman, Amir and Shahrukh Khan amongst male stars to Hema Malini and Aishwarya Rai and many other women stars for their talent and beauty. The strong and independent roles played by women in Indian and south Indian cinema are also serve to promote women's rights. These icons boost India's image enormously and should serve as cultural ambassadors. Indian music and dance too have admirers across the world and more cultural events need to be held amongst our South East Asian and East Asian partners.

Conclusion

The author has been a student of China since 1979 since she was a young undergraduate and has been privileged to see the transformation of China since 1982, when she first went to study in China. At the personal level, the author has travelled across the country, been treated with great hospitality, made good friends and loved the culture, its paintings, porcelain, poetry and architecture, its cuisine and its history. China was, and is, truly one of the grand world civilizations. She has also been impressed by the enormous hard work and patience of the Chinese people despite suffering great personal hardship and loss. They deserve the credit for transforming China from a rural back water to a strong nation state and should be seen as embodying a will to change and succeed that defines modern China.

Yet the author has always noted the lack of freedom, the fear factor in terms of open conversations, the growing inequalities and the coercive, draconian power of the Party state apparatus that force compliance and silence. She has been grateful for the freedoms of India. This is perhaps China's biggest weakness, the lack of its democratic freedoms. Hongkong since 2019, the suppression once again of Democratic rights and calls for democracy by the CCP shows this as the underbelly of the Chinese CCP and the Chinese state historically. Democracy has always been a failed demand put down by state violence since times immemorial. The execution of Qiu Qin in 1909 and the takeover of the nascent democratic politics of 1911 by Yuan Shikai and then Jiang Kaishek in 1927, the single party totalitarianism of the Communist Party since 1949, make this an aborted dream. A dream that alas has always cost the lives of its youth from May 1919 to Tian Anmen 1989 and Hongkong 2019-20.

This is India's strength. Its constitutional democracy, the separation of powers between the judiciary, the legislature and executive and above all freedom of expression, a free media and civil rights. We must guard this great system, despite all its faults, as democracies suffer across the world from Turkey to the USA. India's exceptionalism, its diversity, linguistic and religious and yet, its continued economic growth and modernization, makes it a model that can provide an alternative to totalitarianism as a panacea for development. Today, India is amongst the fastest growing economies, a space power, a technological capacity builder and still a democracy. We must leverage this strength for the greater good of humanism and public participation in decision making internationally.

With regard to the Sino-Indian relationship, the author believes that both countries are destined competitors, as they represent different political systems and economic strategies. However, this competition can be minimized and managed. For India this means working on our multiple strengths while allowing China space within the economic sphere. Perhaps playing the balancing game that we play so well, as we have ably demonstrated over the Ukraine crisis, is our best bet. However, this is not the old cold war between the USA and the Soviet Union, that only affected India tangentially. China's policy in South Asia alone, mandate that India think seriously of peacefully confronting China, if not internationally, then at least in its own neighborhood, in a region with which it shares a long history and cultural past. India has neglected its regional partners and fallen behind China in terms of infrastructure development and economic partnerships and this situation must be rapidly ameliorated. India must have no illusions about China's attempts to contain India's rise. It will always oppose India's membership of the Security council and challenge India's status as a nuclear power. But China is also a pragmatic nation and knows that pushing India into the strategic arms of a strong western alliance will not help it maintain its own regional supremacy. In any case, full blown conflict must be avoided at all costs but we must be ready in case we are called upon to meet this challenge. Here India's growing economic confidence, military alliances and enormous soft power can all work jointly as an effective forward strategy.

Index

W

X

Y

Z